T0150349

I FEEL TO BELIEVE

ABOUT RUNAGATE PRESS

Runagate Press was founded in 1996 by Kalamu ya Salaam and Ayo Fayemi-Robinson (formerly Kysha N. Brown). The press was borne from the influence and inspiration of NOMMO Literary Society, a New Orleans-based black writers' workshop which Salaam founded after Brown questioned the exclusion of women writers from a previous workshop he led at the request of a local university. During the weekly workshops and monthly public readings at Community Book Center, the need to publish was apparent. With the literary contributions of NOMMO writers, the proofreading and editing support of core members, and Salaam's network of writers from across the African Diaspora, the first anthology from Runagate, *Fertile Ground*, received critical acclaim. Runagate Press is dedicated to promulgating New Orleans culture and African heritage cultures worldwide.

I FEEL TO BELIEVE

collected columns

by Jarvis DeBerry

UNIVERSITY OF NEW ORLEANS PRESS
RUNAGATE PRESS

Manufactured in the United States of America
ISBN: 978-1-60801-185-8
University of New Orleans Press
2000 Lakeshore Drive
New Orleans, Louisiana 70119

Cover photo by Frankie Prijatel
Book and cover design by Alex Dimeff

Library of Congress Cataloging-in-Publication Data
Names: DeBerry, Jarvis, author.
Title: I feel to believe : collected columns / Jarvis DeBerry.
Other titles: Columns. Selections | Times-picayune.
Description: First edition. | New Orleans : University of New
Orleans Press, 2020.
Identifiers: LCCN 2020006585 (print) | LCCN 2020006586 (ebook) |
ISBN 9781608011858 (paperback) | ISBN 9781608011919 (epub) |
ISBN 9781608011919 (adobe pdf)
Classification: LCC PN4874.D396 A25 2020 (print) |
LCC PN4874.D396 (ebook) | DDC 814/.6--dc23
LC record available at https://lccn.loc.gov/2020006585
LC ebook record available at https://lccn.loc.gov/2020006586

Printed on acid-free paper
First edition

UNIVERSITY OF NEW ORLEANS PRESS
unopress.org

RUNAGATE PRESS

For my mother, who passed on her love of language, and for my father, who's always believed I'm the best at everything. For Kelly and Naomi, whose love stretches me and lifts me up. And for New Orleans, the city that will always be home.

CONTENTS

ABOUT THE TITLE

When I first arrived in New Orleans, I thought that many black New Orleanians I was hearing were saying that they *failed* to believe a certain thing. But that didn't make sense—because the more I listened, the more I realized they were actually expressing support, not skepticism. They weren't failing to believe something but *feeling* to believe it. "I feel to believe" expresses strong agreement: not just a belief that resides in the head or a feeling that resides in the heart, but the merger of the two, the assertion that one's head and heart are aligned.

ACKNOWLEDGMENTS

This book of columns published in The Times-Picayune wouldn't exist if The Times-Picayune hadn't first taken a chance on me. At the end of my Summer 1997 internship, as I was interviewing with editors Lynn Cunningham, Peter Kovacs and Jim Amoss for a full-time reporting position, I acknowledged that I had far more potential than experience and hoped they would give me the opportunity. They did, and I will forever be grateful.

I'm grateful, too, for all the editors who took notice of me, spoke highly of my work and helped me improve: David Meeks, Bob Warren, Ron Thibodeaux and Robert Rhoden. Though she was never my direct editor, I appreciate Andrea Shaw for always having my back, for talking me through my moments of self-doubt and for being the mentor I needed in the newsroom.

I appreciate former publisher Ashton Phelps Jr. for approving of my being hired to write editorials after a mere two years as a reporter, but he wouldn't have had anything to approve if Terri Troncale hadn't been bold enough to ask. She was the first person at The Times-Picayune to tell me that I had the talent to write opinions, and after hiring me to write editorials, she slowly and methodically helped me fulfill my dream of becoming a columnist.

Outside the paper, I'm grateful for the NOMMO Literary Society, led by one of New Orleans' premier intellectual heavyweights and one of its most prolific writers, Kalamu ya Salaam. Those Tuesday evening workshops (sometimes lasting as long as 6 hours) were invaluable to my development as a writer and to my assimilation into the culture of New Orleans. Special thanks also go out to Vera Warren Williams and Mama Jennifer Turner at Community Book Center for hosting the Friday evening NOMMO readings and for always being so kind and welcoming to me. Many thanks, also, to the people at Christian Unity Baptist Church for helping New Orleans feel like home and for giving me immediate and unvarnished feedback for my work.

I appreciate Abram Himelstein at University of New Orleans Press and Kalamu ya Salaam and Ayo Fayemi-Robinson at Runagate Press for wanting to do this book and for being patient with me as we pulled it together.

My mother, the late Pennie Mae Winfrey DeBerry, was correcting my grammar even as I was learning to talk, and every editor I've had can thank her for her fastidiousness. She was my first and best English teacher, and she and my father, Melvin DeBerry, always made me feel like I could compete with anybody. But it takes a village to raise a reader, and there were multiple people who helped nurture my love of language, including my Aunt Malena Dow, my Uncle Roy DeBerry Jr., Fergenia Hood, and the late Mary Ollie, librarian at Holly Springs Intermediate School.

I started writing columns before I got married and had a family, but Kelly and Naomi both have played a huge role in my work. Some columns I've been scared to write, but I wrote them because I wanted my daughter to have a record of where I stood. I don't want her to guess if I'd taken a position on the tough issues of the day; I want her to see that I did. And as for this collection, Kelly saw the importance of it long before I did. Without her vision, this book wouldn't exist.

INTRODUCTION

A 21-year-old college graduate from a small town in the Deep South wants to be a writer. He moves to New Orleans, fertile ground for literary endeavors.

You've heard this before. As editor of The Times-Picayune, I hired many journalists who matched that profile. But none like Jarvis DeBerry.

He grew up in Holly Springs, Mississippi, population 7,600, near the Tennessee border. He graduated from Washington University in St. Louis, then moved to New Orleans to follow a girl. He was smitten, with the girl and with the city. The girl moved on. Jarvis stayed.

In the summer of 1997, we hired him. He came across as curious and shy, with an irresistible smile and flashes of a wicked sense of humor. He started as an intern in our newsroom, then became a full-time reporter in one of our suburban bureaus.

What he really wanted was to be a columnist. At a staff party that fall, he spoke to editorial page editor Terri Troncale about his dream.

"I told him it was pretty rare to get an opening for a columnist," Terri recalls. "I said, 'Why don't you write some op-eds for me when you feel inspired?'"

A few months later, Jarvis submitted the masterful piece that begins this collection—his argument as a black man that the Merriam-Webster's Collegiate Dictionary should not drop the word "nigger." Beginning with its opening paragraph, the column grabs you and holds you:

"I am not a nigger. I know this because one fall afternoon when I was 7 years old, my father told me I wasn't."

The subject matter is inherently difficult, easily mangled in the hands of an ordinary writer. Instead, Jarvis deconstructs the word's use and effect, its possible contexts, its degrees of impact on black and white speakers, its power to wound, amuse, even endear.

He immerses himself in the nuance and ugliness of the word. He and his 9-year-old black classmates, Jarvis wrote, "had received the hateful definition of the word with our mother's milk, and some of us had already begun to use it ourselves. Some of us had already been lured in, trapped, by the word and all its perverse beauty."

The piece needed hardly any editing. It was a stunning debut. Terri thought Jarvis already had a fully formed writer's voice. She praised him. Then she asked, "Have you ever thought about being an editorial writer?"

Here's Jarvis's summary of their exchanges over several months:

> Quite foolishly, I said, "No."
>
> I mean, I dreamed of being a columnist but an editorial writer? No thanks. MLK holiday, I wrote another column; she praised it and said, "Again, have you ever thought about being an editorial writer?"
>
> I compound the foolishness of my previous response.
>
> I write back, "No, I like having my name on things too much. I don't see how editorial writers get the same ego boost folks with bylines do." Seriously, I was so proudly dumb.
>
> She retorts, "The ego boost comes when people do what you tell them to do."
>
> Me to myself: "Oh."

Eventually, we had an opening. Jarvis talked himself into applying. We—Terri, publisher Ashton Phelps and I—quickly talked ourselves into making the move. Terri set a gradual pace. In addition to editorial writing, Jarvis could write a column every other Friday. Then it became every Friday.

Then came Hurricane Katrina. As we sat dazed in our makeshift Baton Rouge offices, we agreed that Jarvis's voice had to be heard—loud and often. We asked him to write three times a week. He did. Overnight the storm had destroyed his neighborhood and rendered him homeless. Overnight he transformed himself into a full-fledged newspaper columnist.

I write this having just re-read Jarvis's columns. I marveled again at their power, their truth, their honesty, their insight, their courage. As I read, I kept underlining sentences, circling paragraphs.

Jarvis, in the face of national criticism, on why New Orleans would dare celebrate Carnival months after Katrina:

> We are alive. Ask us how our thoughts could turn to celebration after we've suffered so much, how we could think about Mardi Gras even as we continue to suffer, and that's the only answer we can provide. We are alive…
>
> We who had death lapping at our ankles. We who had to crane our necks for the next breath. We who hacked our way out of our attics. We who returned to homes that were muddy and moldy, homes that had fallen down, homes that had been washed off their foundations and had moved on down the street.

Jarvis, in the wake of Charlottesville, on the need to remove Confederate monuments:

> There should be no more debating about whether these monuments that blight the South are actually "white supremacist monuments." Their defenders have loudly objected to that characterization. But it should be plain now to them and to everybody else that white supremacist monuments are what they were meant to be. It's what they are, and it's why they must be removed.

Jarvis on writing "dangerous columns":

> There have been times when a colleague has predicted that a column about to be published will get me in trouble. I've laughed and said, "What good is a columnist who doesn't get in trouble?"

Over 21 years, Jarvis's voice has resonated, sometimes thundered, across our readership, nursed our city through near-death and helped it build a new image of itself. These columns and that voice transcend New Orleans and the South and are spoken with a penetrating eloquence. They deserve the widest audience.

—Jim Amoss, Former Editor
The Times-Picayune

KEEPING A HATEFUL WORD INSIDE A DICTIONARY

JUNE 23, 1998

I am not a nigger. I know this because one fall after-noon when I was 7 years old, my father told me I wasn't.

It did not matter, he told me, how those two white boys up the road had just greeted me; that word did not describe who or what I was. He didn't use that famous "sticks and stones" line; he knew the word could hurt. He just begged me to stop crying and told me repeat-edly what a good person I was.

I remember that day not only for what those two little boys said to me but also because it was the first time I realized that my father was not invincible. His little boy had been hurt, and even though he tried in vain to go find those boys' parents and demand an apology, he told me years later that he realized then that there was nothing he could do to ease my pain.

Last month the publishers of the Merriam-Webster Dictionary announced that despite protests by the NAACP and black parents across the country, they would not remove "nigger" from future editions of their collegiate dictionary. The dictionary currently defines the word as "a black person usu. taken to be offensive" and follows with a paragraph explaining that the word "ranks as perhaps the most offensive and inflammatory racial slur in English. Its use by and among blacks is not always intended or taken as offensive, but it is otherwise a word expressive of racial hatred and bigotry."

Two black women in Michigan, one of whom is a curator of the Museum of Afrikan American History in Flint, started the protests late last year. It's easy to understand why. They don't want to see their children wince while trying to figure out why the word exists. They don't want to have the talk with their children that my father had with me.

But even though I've been stung by the word, even though I'll never forget the look in my father's eyes when I told him what I had just been called, I cannot support the word's removal from one of the most widely read dictionaries of the English language. Merriam-Webster did not invent the word "nigger," but they would be bending to unfair political pressure to pretend that the word does not exist or that it has been used for any other purpose than to a refer to a black or dark-skinned person.

"Anybody can be a nigger," my Sunday school teacher once told our class. She said the word actually describes someone who is "black-hearted," a person equally stupid and evil. Therefore, she told the room of 9- and 10-year-olds, the word is just as apt at describing some white people.

It was an admirable attempt to boost our self-esteem, but I don't know a single kid in my class who believed her.

We knew. Maybe others in my class had been stunned to tears by another child's cruelty. Or maybe their parents and grandparents had told them how the word was lobbed at their souls like Molotov cocktails as they sat in, walked out, stood up and marched for their rights in 1960s Mississippi.

Anyway, we knew. We had received the hateful definition of the word with our mother's milk, and some of us had already begun to use it ourselves. Some of us had already been lured in, trapped, by the word and all its perverse beauty.

Yes. Perverse and beautiful. Hate-inspired, one of the indestructible vestiges of historical racism, it's one of the few words capable of adding injury to insult, making even the most impotent of threats caustic.

But yet, it's beautiful. No, not in the poetic sense but in its multiplicity of functions. As a writer, I am not aware of any other word capable of expressing so many contradictory emotions. Like the blank tile on the Scrabble board, its function depends entirely on the user.

As a junior in high school, I watched my friend as he and a white classmate were engaged in a nasty verbal conflict. All of a sudden, my friend balled his fists and said, "I'm waiting for you to call me a nigger." He knew and I knew that that was the only word he needed to hear to unleash his fists.

But for the young black man struggling to show his appreciation, calling another black man "my nigger" expresses love without sentimentality. For the black person taking a stab at being hip, the word adds an extra pinch of braggadocio. And when we are alone, no other word can express our disappointment in one another like that word can.

However it's used, the word "nigger" drastically changes the tone of a sentence. With so many uses, it might just be the most versatile and most widely applied intensifier in the English language.

Rare is the black person who can convince me that he or she has never used the word either for comedic or dramatic effect. Rarer still is that person who thinks using the word is right. We know its use is indefensible, and we know white Americans who have not and cannot walk in our shoes will never understand how we can simultaneously love comedian Chris Rock and hate former Los Angeles cop Mark Fuhrman. Maybe when black people themselves stop using the word, a national black radio host told his listeners, lexicographers will take note and omit it.

But if a miracle happened tomorrow and all black people refused to ever use the word again, it would be academically unsound for lexicographers to ignore the word's existence. "A dictionary is a scholarly reference, not a political tool," said Deborah Burns, marketing director for Merriam-Webster. "As long as the word is in use, it is our responsibility as dictionary publishers to put the word into the dictionary."

The company did say, though, that they would do a better job at flagging the word as offensive and will place an italicized warning before it and about 200 other inflammatory words it currently defines.

Kathryn Williams, the museum curator who started one of the petitions, had pushed Merriam-Webster for the removal of all hateful language from the dictionary. "If the word is not there, you can't use it," she said.

I disagree. Hate is transmitted by word of mouth, not by the thin, fragile pages of a collegiate dictionary. And denying the word's existence or modifying its definition will neither destroy its shameful history nor numb its venomous sting.

The two boys who insulted me didn't need a dictionary entry to hurt me that day. I didn't need one to understand. Neither do I need one now to tell me who or what I am.

OUTRAGE ERUPTS AFTER DIALLO VERDICT
Fear is no excuse for a killing

MARCH 3, 2000

If Amadou Diallo had grown up in the United States, he would still be alive.

I'm sure it sounds callous to suggest that the Guinean immigrant didn't spend enough time in America, considering that his body was punctured by 19 bullets fired at him by four plainclothes New York cops. But I'm convinced he would still be alive had he been raised here.

Why? Because Diallo, who was innocently standing in front of his home when he was shot, would have had the same scabbed-over wounds on his psyche that every black native son has. He would have long been numb to the idea of being the suspect, of matching the description, of being presumed guilty even in the absence of a crime.

Diallo would have recognized the nervous energy in armed white men and known from experience to keep his cool.

Most importantly, had Amadou Diallo been raised as a black man in America, he would have known what not to do with his hands.

But Amadou had the outrageous misfortune of growing up in Guinea, a black nation run by black people, and didn't arrive here until 1997. He couldn't have known how many assumptions Americans would make at the sight of him.

That ignorance probably cost him his life.

In 1903, W.E.B. Du Bois, a black Harvard-educated sociologist, coined the phrase "double-consciousness," putting into words that strange sensation a black man in America has of "always looking at (himself) through the eyes of others."

Du Bois saw double-consciousness as a burden, and it is. But Amadou Diallo's death demonstrates that it can also be a survival mechanism. Had he been blessed with the burden of double-consciousness, he would have seen himself through the eyes of the cops and known that they saw him as a threat.

The four officers who fired 41 bullets at Diallo were acquitted of murder a week ago after they told jurors they shot him because they feared for their lives. Sadly, they probably were afraid, but that fear likely preceded the moment Diallo pulled out the wallet that they claimed looked like a gun. Even if their alleged fear was a lie, how hard could it be to convince a jury that an innocent black man nonetheless looked threatening?

Truth is, this country looks at the black man in much the same way it looks at the pit bull. Theoretically, each is capable of good behavior, but is it ever really safe to let your guard down? Amadou Diallo was killed in the vestibule of his own apartment building not because of anything he did but because officers thought he had the potential to do something violent.

On two occasions, a nervous white man with a gun on his hip has accused me of having a weapon. When two cops in Mandeville pulled me over and I reached for my registration, one of them yelled, "Keep away from that knife!"

There is something not right in me, or any other black man, having to know how to keep a police officer calm. But I might have been shot had I moved my hand any closer toward the spoon I had carelessly tossed into my glove compartment after eating ice cream.

Just like I might have been shot outside my office building one Saturday afternoon as I arrived for work. When I gathered my things and headed toward the building, the security guard in the parking place next to me asked whether that was a gun I had just put in my pocket.

I laughed at the absurdity of his question, until I saw that he was serious—and nervous. Every reporter at this paper wears a black pager, but only my pager looked like the butt of a gun.

Black friends have had similar experiences. They've found themselves mistaken for burglars, rapists or just your average good-for-nothings. A college classmate who was retrieving boxes he had stored at a friend's apartment suddenly found himself surrounded by six police cruisers. The officers who got out of those cars all had their weapons drawn.

It doesn't matter that we don't have criminal records. We grow up in this country knowing what not to do with our hands.

Someone will surely respond to this column with a stack of statistics. They will tell me that black men commit a disproportionate number of violent crimes.

I know that. And I choose not to make excuses for those who do. I am simply stating what some people in America choose to ignore: Most black men are not criminals.

Most of us are as innocent as Amadou Diallo, and we shudder at the message the Albany jury sent: that it's OK to shoot down an innocent man as long as that man is black.

Amadou Diallo's killers were acquitted because Americans believe that fearing the black man is not so much racism as it is good sense.

It does not matter how blameless he is or whether he's minding his business at home. The jury sanctioned the idea that simply being afraid of a black man is reason enough to kill him.

IF YOU SHAKE IT, YOU WON'T MISTAKE IT

MAY 9, 2003

Most of them would probably be embarrassed if I revealed their names. After all, they are New Orleans' Talented Tenth, those black entrepreneurs, educators and professionals whose accomplishments are supposed to inspire the masses and move the whole race forward. That's how the theory goes, at least.

What then were these movers and shakers doing at a United Negro College Fund black-tie fund-raiser dancing to Juvenile's "Back That Azz Up"?

Well, moving it and shaking it. That's what they were doing.

Please don't mistake my observation for criticism. More than a passive observer, I was out on the floor backing it up, too. I admit to being slowed down, though, at the sight of so many "respectable" New Orleanians dancing suggestively. The silver-haired woman next to me hitched her beaded evening gown up to her knees so she could back it up more ferociously. And suddenly, the men her age had become just as nimble.

DJ Captain Charles was close to reading my mind when he yelled out, "Boy, if y'all's children could see y'all now." Only I thought he should have said, "grandchildren."

Authorship of the song was disputed in federal court this month. DJ Jubilee, known as one of the pioneers of New Orleans' bounce music, released a song called "Back That Ass Up" in 1997. He and his label, Positive Black Talk, Inc., sued rapper Juvenile and Cash Money Records for releasing "Back That Azz Up" in 1998.

I can understand why DJ Jubilee is upset. The song he released in 1997 was a huge hit by local standards. It featured kids shouting out the names of their high schools and zodiac signs when prompted by Jubilee. It also gave them the opportunity to do a sequence of dance steps whose names and moves were known only in New Orleans. The song got continuous airplay on radio station Q93 the summer after its release.

On paper, it might appear that Juvenile and Cash Money Records did nothing more than change Jubilee's two s's to z's, similar to what the group Tag Team did when they followed the group 95 South's song "Whoot, There It Is" with their own called "Whoomp! (There It Is)." But that would be selling Juvenile and producer Mannie Fresh short.

They created a new song, and though the words in the chorus were identical, they took on a new, sexualized meaning that had women shaking their butts with abandon. Jubilee had created a hit. Juvenile and Mannie Fresh had created a national phenomenon.

Captain Charles said Thursday he's been deejaying parties for 21 years. "I've never seen a song that has an impact the way that song has," he said of Juvenile's song. He's seen it move people from "2 years old (to) folks 75 years old."

Not only young and old danced to that record but professionals and blue-collar workers, feminists and misogynists, and according to Captain Charles, black people and white people. He's discovered that Juvenile's song works, "No matter where you play it at."

DJ Jubilee and his label lost their bid in federal court, but to be honest, the jury was never really out. Folks on the dance floor would never get the two songs confused. Nor would the professionals I saw at the UNCF function ever be pulled out to the floor by Jubilee's record.

I told Captain Charles I figured that he used Juvenile's song when he wanted to elevate a great party to a fever pitch. He agreed.

"I start 'em off slow. Then I go for the kill. I knew that particular song at that particular time would do it. It didn't fail, did it?"

BLACK LEADERSHIP HAS BEEN DISCONNECTED

MARCH 19, 2004

I was flipping through the phone book Wednesday afternoon searching for a listing for Black Leadership.

"That's odd," I said to myself. "No listing in the B's or the L's."

I couldn't find African-American Leadership, either, so I called information.

"What city?"

"New Orleans"

"What listing?"

"Black Leadership."

There was a snicker. A cough. A very noisy throat clearing, and then…

A syrupy, professional voice: "I'm sorry. What city did you say?"

"New Orleans."

This time I had to wait a full minute for the laughter to die down. "Gayle, Charlene, Teresa, some guy on the phone wants a listing for Black Leadership!"

"Tell him to get a history book!" I heard one of the women exclaim.

"Y'all aren't being very professional," I said.

"You aren't being very realistic," she said.

"But I see all these people out there talking about black stuff. Aren't they leaders?" I said.

"Shoot, I talk about black stuff all day long. Gayle, Charlene and Teresa can tell you that. But the folks getting the most attention these days aren't leading. They're tearing down folks they don't like. Leadership ain't that petty. It ain't that spiteful."

"But some of them are ministers," I told her. "Sounds like you're encouraging black folks to contradict our spiritual leaders." I figured that would steer her off her blasphemous path.

"No, baby, follow your minister on matters spiritual. Follow him when he stands on principle. Watch out, though, if he demands that you like the politicians he likes. If you're voting age, you can think for yourself. Or can't you?"

"Yeah, I can, but—"

"But what?"

She was frustrating me.

"I can't speak for all the ministers," I said, "and not all of them speak for one another, but some say they're tired of what they say is the larger community's selective outrage—you know, black people getting criticized for doing things they say white folks have always done."

"White folks have gotten away with a whole lot of stuff I'd warn black folks not to try," she said. "I'm not saying it's fair. But we ain't supposed to envy folks doing wrong. I've read that someplace. Proverbs, I think."

"Careful, now," I warned her. "Scripture-quoting contests can get real ugly."

"No uglier than blackness contests," she said, "but there are some pots out there determined to prove the kettle less black."

"Aha! So you're a Nagin supporter," I told her. "Either that or some type of conservative. I knew you'd eventually out yourself."

"Baby, my vote is up for grabs. If the folks we've talked about want to talk about the mayor's record and honestly hold it up against those who came before him, I'm all ears. I might even agree with 'em on some things. But who's to judge a blackness contest? Tell me quick: Who's blacker? Allen Iverson or Arthur Ashe?"

"Well, if I had to choose, I'd say..."

"Too late. Time's up."

"You're tough."

"No, baby, I'm real." She started laughing. "That's a joke you wouldn't get. That's my last name: R-I-L-L. First name Beatrice."

"Bea Rill, huh? Cute."

"Yes, I'm that, too. And my family has always kept our politics simple and logical."

"So Ms. Bea, are you telling me that my search for Black Leadership is fruitless?"

"No, baby, I'm telling you to lead your own black self."

AS IF BLACK PEOPLE WANT TO BE TERRORIZED

JULY 1, 2005

People tend to act in their own self-interest. If you find a group of people who don't, you can safely assume that they are acting in what they perceive to be their self-interest.

That should be a fairly easy concept to grasp. Easy even for Harry Lee.

But the truth still eludes him. The Jefferson Parish sheriff suggested Monday that black people are morally deficient and would rather be terrorized by criminals than live in safety.

"Blacks don't turn in blacks," he blathered at a press conference that he called to decry the crime problems in New Orleans. "There's something in their culture that they don't turn in a brother."

That lie would have been enough, but the sheriff decided that while he was spouting nonsense, he might as well lie about white people, too.

White people don't have drug problems in their neighborhoods, he said. The reason they don't? They turn each other in as soon as they suspect something's amiss.

Reader, I know what you're thinking. You're thinking, "Hey, wasn't there a big drug scandal within the ranks of the sheriff's office last year? Didn't the mug shots of deputies accused of distributing drugs, using drugs or covering up drug activity show the faces of white people?"

You're also remembering the sheriff's comment at the Sept. 29 press conference he called to announce the firings or resignations of those involved. He said, "They've lost their careers, in my opinion, because of their stupidity, because of their allegiance to each other instead of to the people of Jefferson Parish."

It's funny, isn't it? Not even a year has gone by, and the problem with witnesses not reporting crime has become a failing exclusive to the black community. It wasn't long ago that Sheriff Lee forced out of his department white people who used and trafficked in drugs, but now he announces that white communities are uniformly clean.

The deputies who didn't report the wrongdoing they saw were no doubt acting in what they thought to be their best interest. Informants are usually branded snitches, and they are paid back with insults, alienation and sometimes threats.

If a gun-carrying officer of the law can be too timid to step forward, what do we expect from civilians who might legitimately fear that they'll be harmed if they report the crimes they see?

Some murder witnesses in New Orleans have been killed. Some murder suspects have been acquitted—even though their innocence is very much in doubt. The city's law enforcement agencies haven't always done a good job working together—to the peril of the communities they're sworn to protect.

Yet, Lee says it's the blackness that's the problem. There's a cultural flaw that prevents black people from turning in a "brother."

That's ridiculous. No victim of any race calls a criminal "brother." Furthermore, there are safe black neighborhoods all over this metropolitan area. They stay safe because suspicious activity is reported and because neighbors unite against criminals of every color.

Black people have what everybody else has: an instinct for self-preservation. Innocent witnesses who don't talk make that decision because they don't believe the police or the district attorney will keep them safe. So they hope their silence will.

It's not a smart strategy. But it is one that's easily understood. Silence doesn't necessarily protect, but then again, neither does speaking up. But when law enforcement officials demonstrate that every witness who works with them will be kept safe and every suspect who needs to go to jail will go, then can we expect witnesses to report criminals with regularity.

At that point, witnesses will see that their self-interest and the interests of their neighborhoods are identical.

VIOLENCE TESTS THE LIMITS OF MORTICIAN'S ART

AUGUST 26, 2005

It's the rare businessman who wishes his business were slower. But it's easy to understand why Malcolm Gibson does. He works in New Orleans as a mortician. Brisk business equals violent streets.

As co-owner of Professional Funeral Services, Gibson gets bodies that have been so perforated by bullets that it's a challenge just to keep the embalming fluid inside. Sometimes the jawbones have been shattered, and the face no longer has the shape of a face.

Nevertheless, the mothers of the victims give Gibson a demand: "I want to see my son the way he was before this happened."

That's not easy to do. "If you can imagine a bullet hole in the center of somebody's forehead," Gibson said Thursday morning. "You can't leave it that way."

Gibson, 35, became fascinated with mortuary science at age 10 when he saw his grandfather's body in a casket. The man's death from bone cancer had been agonizing. Yet, the mortician restored to the body a look of peace. That peaceful look not only helped him accept his grandfather's passing, Gibson told me, but it also inspired him. He wanted to know how that mortician did what he did so he could do the same thing for others.

But there are limitations to what he can do. It's hard to make a face torn apart by bullets look like something other than a face torn apart by bullets. If the person doesn't die instantly, there's going to be swelling. If it's a hot New Orleans day or night and the body isn't quickly discovered, the deterioration process will begin.

Still, grieving mamas want a picture-perfect body to lay out in the church.

Gibson said he tries not to become numbed by the never-ending train of dead bodies. Then again, a certain amount of empathy is inevitable.

"Most of the murder victims look like me," he said. "They're black men."

But that's not the only person they look like. Sometimes he's working on the body of a young person, and "for a minute I'll see my son's face."

Gibson's 15-year-old son no doubt knows the legend of the rapper 50 Cent, whose claim to authenticity is that he was shot nine times and survived. Gibson knows it, too. That's why he's brought his son with him to work, so he can see the much more common and unglamorous result of street-level warfare.

His son says to him, "Oh, Daddy, it stinks!"

He replies, "Yes, that's the stench of death."

"It's one thing to hear (about) it on TV," he said. "It's another thing to see a body riddled with bullets. It's not a cartoon."

To hear Gibson tell it, one need only go to the funeral of a victim to know that murder begets murder. He's seen people stand over caskets and promise to strike down the murderer. Mourners almost always know who the murderer is, he told me, though they rarely trust police enough to tell them about it. Instead, they make sure the murderer soon inhabits a casket of his own.

What he finds particularly disturbing are the people who've come to accept murder as a necessary part of life. He once heard a woman scream out at a funeral, "They couldn't even kill you like a man! They had to sneak up on you."

The murder itself was the tragedy, but, Gibson said, the woman seemed to think that her loved one's death would have been more acceptable if his murderers had behaved honorably and squared off with him first.

"It's business," he said about the preparation and funerals of murder victims, "but there's enough business that if I never had another, I'd be OK."

ONCE YOU FALL, YOU'LL NEVER BE THE SAME

SEPTEMBER 16, 2005

Black people have a phrase for the kind of love that's indistinguishable from stupidity. The person so afflicted is said to have his "nose open." If my nose hadn't once been as wide open as a canyon, I may never have set foot in New Orleans.

When people ask me how I ended up in New Orleans, I usually say "a job." It's true that an internship with The Times-Picayune gave me an official excuse to be in the city, but it wasn't the job that drew me to the place. I came to New Orleans for a woman, a woman who had been sending plenty of signals that she didn't want me anymore. I pursued her anyway. Stupidity has never been so richly rewarded.

I had been to New Orleans three times before my internship began and had hated the place more with each successive trip. I blamed New Orleans for my girlfriend's waning affection. I felt boring. That wasn't a new feeling at all, but I thought my boringness must have seemed all the more conspicuous to her contrasted against the neon lights of Bourbon Street. New Orleans was stealing my woman, and I hated the place the way I'd hate any romantic competitor.

Still, I moved in. If New Orleans was where the battle for her heart was being waged, I needed to be on the front line. But wouldn't you know it? She's the one who eventually left the city, and I'm the one now writing love songs to it.

New Orleans attracts tourists because of its perceived exoticism. But I chose to call it home because its traditions felt so natural. On return trips to my birthplace in northern Mississippi, I've tried to greet family and friends with a kiss on the cheek. They're expecting a stiff-armed handshake. A place where people don't hug hello now feels foreign to me. Not just foreign but backwards.

New Orleanians are sometimes criticized for being uninhibited folk. Granted, there's value in some inhibitions—and it would be nice if the city's tourists would observe some now and then—but New Orleanians figured out long ago that emotional restraint and stoicism just aren't natural. Consequently, grown men aren't afraid to call other grown men "baby," and mourners can dance at a relative's funeral without fear of being thought undignified. In fact, there's a greater chance they'd be talked about if they didn't dance.

One Tuesday evening in Treme, I watched the neighborhood throw a parade for a homeless man. He had passed away behind a nearby funeral home. Everybody knew him. So somebody had the idea that they ought to honor his memory. There are places where highfalutin people don't have parades held in their honor. In New Orleans a homeless man was honored. The crowds wouldn't have danced any more jubilantly if he had had a mailing address in Eastover.

Maybe my nose is as wide open for New Orleans as it used to be for the woman who drew me there*, but when I stood in Treme last week, I found myself silently agreeing with residents who were defying Mayor Ray Nagin's order to leave town. "If I leave New Orleans, where the hell I'm gon' be after that?" a stalwart Robert Thomas asked me. I interpreted his question two ways. He wanted to know to which mystery location he'd be shipped if he consented to leave, and he was also asking how he could possibly make his home somewhere else or why anybody would think he'd agree to such a thing.

Those who left the city weren't exactly agreeing to go. They left because they could see no other way to make it where they were. Some folks seem not to understand that. Barbara Bush said last week that living in a Texas evacuation shelter was no big deal for some New Orleanians because so many of them were underprivileged anyway.

Leaving home under duress would be catastrophic for any human being, but leaving New Orleans is more stressful still. We love that place with all the tenacity, defiance and ferocity we can muster. Others might find our love of the place incomprehensible, but to us, nothing makes more sense.

---

* This column and the two that follow were written at The Times-Picayune's makeshift office in Baton Rouge. Hence, the word "there" and not "here."

THERE IS SOME HONOR AMONG THIEVES

SEPTEMBER 27, 2005

Not the New Orleans Police Department. Not the United States Army. Not the United States Coast Guard or the Louisiana National Guard. Not the New Orleans Fire Department or the Louisiana Department of Wildlife and Fisheries. And certainly not the Federal Emergency Management Agency.

When Vivian Buckner, her mother, Jessie Richardson, and dozens of others huddled at the Lafon Nursing Facility needed relief after Hurricane Katrina, the items they needed to sustain them arrived on a mail carrier's truck. But the occupants were not affiliated with the United States Postal Service.

They were thieves. They had stolen the postal truck and were using it not only to deliver needed supplies to people along Chef Menteur Highway but also to offer rides to the Superdome for those who wanted to go.

I know Buckner and her 94-year-old mother. We all attend the same church. When I called Buckner in Houston Saturday, I teased her for missing the service we had at 7:30 a.m. Aug. 28. By that Sunday morning, though, most people had either fled, were fleeing or had picked the spot where they'd ride out the storm. Buckner had already arrived at the nursing home. She expected to ride out of New Orleans on the same bus that would drive her mother and the other nursing home residents to safety.

Buckner had attended four meetings since April explaining what would be done during an evacuation, she told me. The nursing home had had a practice evacuation. Yet, the buses Buckner was waiting for never came. According to The Washington Post, they weren't requested.

Sister Augustine McDaniel, who runs the Sisters of the Holy Family facility, reportedly decided that it would be better to stay put than to try to leave. Because the state attorney general is investigating how McDaniel handled the crisis, the nun has been advised by an attorney not to talk. Because she witnessed what went on that week, investigators have told Buckner to expect a subpoena.

She told me she witnessed death and despair, a dedicated staff of employees and volunteers trying to save everyone they could and then a stolen mail truck pulling up outside Tuesday.

"First when they came we were really afraid of them," Buckner told me. "We knew the post office wasn't open."

But the people on the truck didn't menace them. Instead, "They said, 'Y'all need anything?'"

Buckner said she and the rest of the ad hoc staff could look through the open door and see what was on the truck: water, juice, potato chips, cookies, peanut butter and crackers. So that became the list of things they needed.

The thieves promised to return, and Wednesday they brought back baby wipes and adult diapers, nightgowns and Gatorade. They also brought back chicken and red beans and rice they'd taken from Popeyes. Buckner told me she didn't know how or when the food had been cooked, but the residents hadn't eaten since Monday, so they had no choice but to serve it. "Everybody ate it," she told me, "and nobody got sick."

The thieves were also good stewards of their loot. "They told us, 'Take whatever you need, but you gotta give us back the rest.'"

She had used the word "they" so often that I finally asked Buckner how many men were on the truck.

"They weren't men," she corrected me. "They were boys."

"Boys?!"

"I don't guess they were over 18," she said. "That's how we knew they didn't work for the postal service." She paused. "They didn't work for nobody."

I tried in vain Monday to reach a spokesperson with the United States Postal Inspection Service. I wanted to know whether the boys who had stolen the truck had been arrested. If so, I wanted to know if the agency was aware that they had used the truck to save lives. Buckner said she saw a car from the postal inspection service drive past on Chef Menteur Wednesday—after the boys had made their delivery. Like almost every other official vehicle she saw that week, that car zoomed by without stopping.

"Everybody passed," she said. "Even the Army trucks passed."

Everybody except two thieves who provided aid when the government did not.

KATRINA ROBBED US OF SO MANY PRECIOUS THINGS

OCTOBER 2, 2005

The Thursday after Hurricane Katrina I was preparing to come to work at The Times-Picayune's new location in Baton Rouge. I was pocketing those things I always pick up before walking out the door: wallet, cell phone, keys.

That's when I stopped. "Keys? What do I have to unlock?"

I laughed the way all of us must have laughed when we've caught ourselves doing things the way we would have done them before the storm. I put the keys in my camera bag, zipped it up and got used to walking around without them.

Four Thursdays later I was still in Baton Rouge, but on this day I knew I'd be going to New Orleans to check on my house. As I was getting ready to leave, I realized with a start that I didn't have my keys. How pathetic would that be, I thought—me enduring Baton Rouge's hellish traffic, driving the 80 miles to New Orleans, only to realize that the keys I needed were back in the capital city?

I needn't have worried. The lock on every exterior door had rusted. The keys were as useless on Sept. 29 as they had been on Sept. 1.

To get inside, I had to do what soldiers had done Sept. 10 when they used neon yellow spray paint to mark my house: I had to climb in through a side window.

The room I landed in looked diseased. Like the black spots that appear on a rotting banana or an onion that's been left too long in the fridge, the mold running up the walls suggested an advanced state of decay. The house is still in the process of dying.

I know that others have gone back to their homes because they want to see whether that one cherished item survived the wind and the water: the framed photo of a deceased relative, a necklace from a spouse, a prized vase or crystal bowl. I thought I had removed from my house everything that was irreplaceable—I hadn't, but I'd told myself I had—so I was there out of a sense of obligation. I was going to have to face the destruction eventually. Why not now?

I headed first for my bedroom. I wonder if that's what everybody who returns will do. The rooms where we sleep define us, and they often house our most precious valuables. Why not start there?

I couldn't get in. I turned the knob, pushed the door with my hand, pushed it with my shoulder and karate-kicked it repeatedly. It never budged.

By contrast, the door to the office across the hall gave way with modest effort. When I say "gave way," understand that I do mean "gave way." After a couple of pushes, my right arm went right through the door. At that point, I pushed the whole door down.

In his famous piece "Areopagitica," John Milton wrote, "(A)s good almost kill a man as kill a good book." I remember debating that statement in my high school English class. Some classmates thought that Milton's position was too over the top to be considered. But I can say now that seeing most of my books in one sodden heap on the floor killed me. All the bookcases had fallen over. The desk had collapsed. The certificates on the walls were destroyed even as they remained attached to the walls.

I didn't stay long. I didn't see the need. I grabbed some books from the top shelf of a built-in case, but that was all. When I saw what looked like white cotton candy growing atop the blades of my ceiling fans, I took it as evidence that the organisms that feast on death and decay had moved in permanently and that I was intruding on them.

Thousands of New Orleanians are chomping at the bit to get back to the city. Their eagerness says to me that they believe something good awaits them there. Many of them will have happier stories than mine. But many of them will have stories as bad. Many will have stories that are worse.

I remembered Thursday night that behind my bedroom door were two quilts my grandmother had made for me. I felt bad for having told friends that I had removed everything that was irreplaceable. I hadn't. I'm guessing that many folks are going to return to their destroyed structures and realize that they hadn't either.

FEMA CHIEF PRIMPED AS A CITY SANK

NOVEMBER 4, 2005

On the Sunday after Hurricane Katrina laid waste to New Orleans and large portions of the Gulf Coast, Sharon Worthy, a press secretary for the Federal Emergency Management Agency, sent her boss, Michael Brown, an e-mail telling him that he needed to roll up his sleeves.

Louisiana would have been well served if Worthy had been speaking figuratively. We would have cheered her on if her e-mail had been an example of a subordinate demanding that her lazy boss get to work and display some leadership.

But we weren't so lucky. Worthy, much like her boss, seemed blissfully unconcerned about the multitudes desperate for help from FEMA. Also like her boss, she was spending an inordinate amount of time worrying about his physical appearance. The e-mail she sent had the subject line "Your shirt." In its entirety:

> *Please roll up the sleeves of your shirt ... all shirts. Even the President rolled his sleeves to just below the elbow.*
>
> *In this crises (sic) and on TV you just need to look more hard working ... ROLL UP THE SLEEVES!*

According to Greek myth, Narcissus was so en-
tranced with his reflection on a lake that he fell in and
drowned. Judging by a series of e-mails Brown sent and
received during and after Hurricane Katrina, he was so
concerned with his physical appearance that he didn't
care that others were drowning.

During a time when every single employee
at FEMA should have been focused on responding to
the need of Katrina's victims, Brown was entertaining
and responding to compliments about his appearance.
Even as the hurricane was coming ashore in coastal
Mississippi, Brown got a fawning e-mail from Cin-
dy Taylor, his deputy director of public affairs. She
told him, "My eyes must certainly be deceiving me.
You look fabulous—and I'm not talking the makeup!"
Brown responded with a speed that suggests he didn't
give a damn about the storm or the people in its path.

He told Taylor that he'd been shopping at Nordstrom.
"Are you proud of me?"

An hour later Brown e-mailed Taylor, public affairs
specialist Michael Widomski and Marty Bahamonde,
a regional FEMA director who was trapped inside the
Louisiana Superdome with yet another comment about
his appearance. "If you'll look at my lovely FEMA attire
you'll really vomit," Brown wrote. "I ama (sic) fashion
god."

The statement that "There were failures at all levels
of government" is misleading because it implies that
ineptitude was evenly distributed from Pennsylvania
Avenue down to Perdido Street. It wasn't. It was con-
centrated at the top.

Michael Brown couldn't pull himself away from his
mirror, his subordinates were lining up to kiss his butt

and President Bush was praising him for the "heck of a job" he was doing.

And people in Louisiana were still dying.

Rep. Charlie Melancon and Rep. Tom Davis of Virginia released the e-mails this week after Secretary of Homeland Security Michael Chertoff responded to their request for documents and communications relating to the federal government's response to Hurricane Katrina.

The e-mails not only reveal Brown's crippling vanity, but when presented side by side with his statements to Congress, they also expose him as an audacious liar.

He claimed that he and his agency responded aggressively to the disaster when the e-mails show the only thing he really responded to were cutesy little compliments about his looks.

WHEN LIFE'S HAVEN TURNS DEATHTRAP

For some of the elderly, nothing—not even a killer hurricane—is more frightening than leaving home

NOVEMBER 6, 2005

Sunday morning my sister sat behind a keyboard leading the local remnant of her congregation in a song by David Frazier and Hezekiah Walker called "I Need You To Survive."

The song is beautifully simple: "I pray for you. You pray for me. I love you. I need you to survive."

As the people around me sang, I remembered the many people who didn't survive. They had relatives who loved them and wanted them to evacuate before Hurricane Katrina made landfall. But many seem to have interpreted their relatives' concern not as love but as interference, and they dug in their heels at home—and died there.

State data indicate that more than 60 percent of Louisianans who died during Hurricane Katrina or immediately after were 61 or older. More than 37 percent were 76 or older. The fact that the elderly have more physical ailments and are less mobile than younger people surely explains many of the deaths. But not all of them. The series of obituaries The Times-Picayune has been running under the headline "Katrina's Lives Lost" makes clear that many elderly victims had a way out. They declined it.

Their younger relatives begged them to leave and offered transportation, but they said no. They'd ridden out storms before, and, like every other hardship they'd faced, this, too, would pass.

When I realized how angry I was becoming at seniors who'd stayed put and died, how I was yelling to friends about their stubbornness, I decided to call Dr. Dan Blazer, president of the American Association for Geriatric Psychiatry. I asked him why, given the dire forecast and the high potential for disaster, so many elderly people would turn down rides to safety.

As counterintuitive as it sounds, Dr. Blazer said, seniors are more likely to want to stay because home—even one in the path of a hurricane—gives them their greatest sense of security.

"Just the idea of going into the unknown is much more threatening to them," he said. "Moving, change, represents insecurity to them, far more so (than) to those of us who are younger."

Blazer said the older person's family might be saying, "A hurricane is coming. We need to get out," but "the older person is saying, 'A hurricane is coming. That's sort of an abstract idea. I feel secure here.'"

Those of us who were raised well were taught to respect our elders. But if respect means we always defer to what they say no matter the circumstance, then that very hierarchy could imperil the elder's life.

"Many times we're forced ... to act like we're the parents of our parents. (That's) a very difficult thing for children to do sometimes," Dr. Blazer said. "Even when they're 85 and you're 60, you just don't want to do it." However, "If your older parent is in some danger, you don't ask. You just go ahead and make the decision and get them out of there.

"Too often we're expecting these older people to act rationally, and that's just not the way they're acting. Sometimes you have to take a stance and do something."

Even if that something makes them furious, he said.

Psychologically speaking, what happens to people as they age is "almost the reversal of what happens in childhood." Dr. Blazer said. Babies cling to their parents for a while before venturing out to explore the world, he said. "In later life you see people pulling in the area where they will venture out closer and closer and closer."

Those of us who see well, hear well and are confident in our ability to walk without falling might not understand how terrifying it is to discover reduced capacity, Dr. Blazer said. But those who realize that their bodies are in decline tend to compensate by "bringing in the boundaries," he said.

They stick to the places where they feel secure. Therefore, it doesn't matter if the suggested evacuation spot is nearby or if it's easy to get there, he said. "The idea of going to Houston seems like going to Timbuktu."

I told Dr. Blazer that I couldn't understand why so many older people chose to stay with their houses. It's as if they thought their presence could steer away the wind and water, I said.

He helped me see that I was wrong to assume that people stayed simply to protect their things.

"In their mind it's all they know," Dr. Blazer said. "It's not just a question of possession. This is my place. I don't know of any other place where I can be."

Katrina won't be the last hurricane to hit New Orleans. And when the next one threatens there will be people—many of them elderly—who will dismiss the notion that they need to be rescued. If we love them, we'll do everything necessary to make sure they survive. They may feel angry and out of place, but those two reactions will be proof that they're alive.

TRIUMPH OVER SORROW IS OUR M.O.

DECEMBER 6, 2005

"come celebrate with me that everyday something
has tried to kill me and has failed."

–Lucille Clifton

*   *   *

We are alive.

Ask us how our thoughts could turn to celebration
after we've suffered so much, how we could think about
Mardi Gras even as we continue to suffer, and that's the
only answer we can provide.

We are alive.

Yes, we've lost things. We've lost homes. Big ones, little
ones, shotguns, camelbacks, cottages, mansions. We've
lost neighborhoods. Rich ones, poor ones, mixed ones.
Loud ones, quiet ones. We've lost schools and congrega-
tions. We've lost jobs. We've lost our sense of community,
our sense of security, and some of us may feel that we've
lost or are losing whatever grip we had on our sanity.

We've lost people. Not just random people, either, but
loved ones: mamas and daddies, marraines and par-
rains, our neighbors, our classmates, grandparents. So
many grandparents.

You ask, "Who in their right minds would think of this as a time to plan a celebration?"

We would.

We who had death lapping at our ankles. We who had to crane our necks for the next breath. We who hacked our way out of our attics. We who returned to homes that were moldy and muddy, homes that had fallen down, homes that had been washed off their foundations and had moved on down the street.

It might not make sense to you. Perhaps you hear our plans and ask, "How could you?" Try to understand. This is what we do. This is who we are. Defiance defines us. And at this time and in this place nothing needs to be more assiduously defied than death itself.

We know how to do that. We created the jazz funeral. Not out of disrespect for the deceased but out of a need to celebrate the life that was lived and a determination to press forward joyfully, no matter how hard life's trials.

Jazz wouldn't have been jazz without the drum. And the drum that sparked its evolution would never have been played if the Africans who were brought here in bondage hadn't decided that they had traditions worth carrying forward. I can imagine that at least one person who was brought over in the hold of a ship felt it inappropriate to drum, to sing, to dance in Congo Square.

But imagine this city, imagine this nation, imagine this world if those original Afro-New Orleanians had let their sorrow—the sorrow over never seeing home or any of their loved ones ever again—completely rob them of the cultures they cherished. New Orleans would never have become the city we all loved.

And it won't be that lovable city again if we don't fight

for our traditions. At a town hall meeting held in Atlanta Saturday, a woman asked Mayor Ray Nagin, "How can we be having Mardi Gras and we aren't even there?" Others say it disrespects the dead. They say it gives outsiders the impression that everything in New Orleans is OK. I say it gives them proof that we aren't dead.

The argument that Feb. 28 is too soon to celebrate assumes that one day our sorrow will expire. It won't. As long as we can remember the people who died, our collective sadness will linger.

Mardi Gras won't abolish that sorrow, no more than the happy music played during second lines obliterates the memory of the departed. But it will announce to the world that that which tried to kill this city did not succeed.

We know what has happened to us. A celebration won't mean we've forgotten. It will let the world know not only that we aren't dead but that we have no intentions of dying.

MAYOR STEPS IN IT, TOTALLY DEEP

JANUARY 20, 2006

"Hey, we didn't get our 40 acres and a mule, but we did get you, C.C."

– Parliament

*   *   *

Black people love Clinton. I thought that was well established. Yet, it came as a shock, made some folks absolutely apoplectic, when on Monday, New Orleans Mayor C. Ray Nagin dipped into Clinton's book of phrases and came up with an especially colorful one: chocolate city.

The blowback must have taken Nagin by surprise. How can Clinton get away with using the phrase for a whole 30 years, but Nagin gets blasted no sooner than the words fell out of his mouth Monday? The mayor probably thought he showed restraint. For example, he didn't suggest that Dave Chappelle be named this country's secretary of education. He didn't suggest that the Rev. Al Sharpton be given control over the U.S. Treasury, and he didn't suggest that Alicia Keys move into the temporarily White House as our next first lady.

But in 1975, Clinton predicted that a similar cast of entertainers would be running things in our chocolate capital, and nobody mounted a protest.

OK, so that was George Clinton, intergalactic funkateer and chief navigator of the Mothership Connection, originator of P-funk and propagator of all things groovy. I doubt Clinton's ever spoken at a Martin Luther King Jr. commemoration. His brain cells have probably never touched down long enough for him to give a coherent address.

But he's always been influential. In 1975, Clinton's band, Parliament, released the album "Chocolate City." On the title track, which reached No. 24 on Billboard's black music chart, we hear Clinton expounding on the growing number of chocolate cities: Newark, New Jersey; Gary, Indiana; Atlanta. He addresses them collectively as "C.C."

"You're my piece of the rock, and I love you, C.C. Can you dig it?"

When that song was released, Nagin would have been a freshman at a chocolate campus, Tuskegee University. Obviously, the song stuck with him, although I'm sure his public relations staff is wishing that it hadn't. They must know that their boss stepped in it—and not just knee-deep.

What the mayor said was dumb. The idea that God cares about New Orleans' racial demographics makes one wonder if the mayor didn't share a few moments backstage with Clinton before coming out to speak. I mean, you've got to be smoking the strong stuff to come up with that one.

However, the subsequent outrage suggests that the comment was interpreted by some people not as the dumb remark it was but as one that was mean-spirited, exclusionary, even hateful. Such interpretations ignore the fact that the mayor was trying to allay concerns that the Bring New Orleans Back Commission and he himself are engaged in a conspiracy to depress the black population. Since his campaign four years ago, Nagin's most vocal opponents have accused him of not being black enough. Remember those ads that said he ought to call himself Ray Reagan? How about the preacher who called him a white man in black skin?

How does a mayor who's had to constantly defend his blackness give a signal that he's not trying to send black people away? The short answer is: not the way he tried to do it Monday. His delivery no doubt made some people wonder if he shouldn't be sent away—to the third floor of Charity.

(By the way, what's going to be our new shorthand for crazy now that Charity Hospital is closed?)

Chocolate City, at least as it is described by Clinton, is not an exclusively black place. It is not a city where white people are barred entry, disenfranchised or treated poorly. Instead, it is a city where, chiefly because of white flight, a majority of those left are black. Chocolate City is New Orleans on Aug. 28, 2005.

I don't know if New Orleans will be a chocolate city again, and I doubt God cares one way or the other. But if most New Orleanians thought immediately of Willy Wonka and not a track from the funkiest band ever— that's all the proof we need that New Orleans isn't a chocolate city now.

OPERATOR'S FULL OF ADVICE, BUT IT'S YOUR CALL

APRIL 7, 2006

I had no idea if she'd made it back to town or if I'd be able to reach her if she had. I made her acquaintance two years ago when, in a moment of frustration and disappointment, I dialed information seeking a listing for Black Leadership.

She, the operator, laughed at me, gave me a lecture on self-reliance and revealed a name that sounded an awful lot like a punch line: Beatrice Rill.

Months later, this same Bea Rill, self-proclaimed information connoisseur, actually called me. I didn't dare ask how she got my number. We talked late into the night about all the phoniness masquerading as political leadership. But then we lost contact.

Had she made it through the storm OK? Was she back? I dialed 411.

"I've been wondering if you were gonna have sense enough to call me," the voice said.

"How'd you know it was me?" I said. Then, "I guess that was a dumb question, huh?"

"And you come off as so smart in the paper," she said.

I ignored that crack. "I wasn't sure if you'd come back," I said.

"I'm needed here," she said. "Gotta offset some of this nonsense. Gotta be here to provide information to folks who need it. You're not the only one who asks me for advice."

"What do folks ask you?"

"Mainly people ask me the same thing you asked a couple of years back: if it says something bad about them if their opinions don't match the ones certain leaders say they should have."

"Black people?"

"Some. But not all. I've had cops call and ask if they're required to pull out that 'but there're some good cops' line every time a bad cop is exposed. I've had folks from so-called good neighborhoods confess that they aren't as bothered by trailers as they are bothered by those bothered by trailers. I've had black folks who've chosen to stay away rankle at being told of their right to return. It ain't about rights for them. They just happen to like it where they are.

"Folks just don't know sometimes how to jibe what they think with what they're supposed to think."

"What do you tell them?"

"I tell 'em my name, baby. Often that's enough. I tell 'em that they've got to live with themselves."

"'To thine own self be true.' Polonius to Laertes. Hamlet. Act 1. Scene 3."

"'Baby, I'm for real. I'm as real as real can get.' The Dramatics. 'Whatcha See is Whatcha Get.' 1971."

"That's before my time," I said.

"So, Shakespeare is your contemporary?"

I fumbled for a response. "It sounds like you should've run for office."

"You insult me."

"How is that an insult?"

"There ain't no place for truth telling in elected office. And there sure isn't any in campaigning. Think about it. How many candidates have you heard say something that made you say, 'Now that's the sho' nuff truth?'"

"Not many."

"I'm gonna ask that question again. 'How many—'"

"OK, OK. You got me. Nobody."

"That means it ain't no place for Bea Rill."

"But we've still gotta vote for somebody," I said. "How do we decide?"

"'We' don't," she said. "Ain't but one person in that booth at a time. Vote as an individual. Trust yourself to know the difference between good and bad, between a strand of carnival beads and granny's pearls. Then don't lose sight of the fact that if you make a mistake and it all turns out wrong, this too shall pass."

OUR INNERMOST SELVES, STREWN ON THE CURB

APRIL 11, 2006

I didn't sleep well Friday night, and I woke up hours before I had planned to rise Saturday morning. I was worried that the people scheduled to help me remove all the contents from my flooded house that morning would look at the mess inside and make unflattering judgments about me.

One's house should be in order before company arrives, and the fact that my house was rarely in order was the reason I rarely had company. If a stranger—or even a good friend—had arrived at my house Aug. 28, I'd have been embarrassed at the mess he'd have seen.

Psychoanalysis would probably reveal that I deliberately kept things messy so as not to face the chore of entertaining guests and that letting people in physically would have been akin to letting them in emotionally. That old cliché about a man's home being his castle is often interpreted as a defense of patriarchy, but perhaps the phrase better explains the strong desire some of us have to wall ourselves off from the rest of the world.

Home is the place where we don't have to explain anything, the place where the stuff we want unseen remains that way, the place where we can live free of judgment if only because there's nobody there to judge.

And yet, on Saturday morning, a group of friends and strangers affiliated with The Times-Picayune were going to show up at my house and see everything. An angel by the name of Suzanne Stouse decided a while back that we who work here ought to organize ourselves and help one another muck out and gut out our flooded homes. My colleagues urged me to put my name on the list.

Stripping away our privacy is one of the many ways Hurricane Katrina humiliated us. We may not have missed a single month's rent, may never have failed to pay the mortgage, and yet, all our worldly possessions still ended up on the curb as if they'd been tossed out by a constable.

Saturday, we were not even permitted the dignity of trash bags.

A woman who drove past in an official-looking fluorescent yellow vest saw the pile of black contractor bags that had accumulated and told us that we would have to empty them all. The debris removal teams have to be able to separate the different kinds of trash, she said. Therefore, everything we'd bagged would have to be shaken out onto the ground.

Everything that was in my drawers, including the drawers I wore. Everything I'd ever bought at the drug store. Old birthday cards. Journals, including some that chronicled my life's most despairing moments. Wine bottles, in-line skates, love letters, boxing gloves, cassette tapes, break-up letters.

All these things and more were handled Saturday by folks who wouldn't have dared to touch them before. Not only were they handled, but all those things and more are now on exhibit to the world.

The work of the writer demands exposure, but we who write are always in control of what and how much we reveal on the page.

On Saturday, editing was not an option.

Laid out before everyone was my life: messy before the storm and infinitely more messy after. One might have called it "Jarvis: The Unauthorized Biography."

At any other time in my life, such an affront to my privacy would have been too much to bear. The only thing that makes it bearable now is the knowledge that there are too many other lives on display out there for any passerby to focus too closely on mine.

SHAKING IT IN THE NEW NEW ORLEANS

APRIL 25, 2006

Sunday morning, I parked in a neighborhood of half-a-million dollar homes to join a second-line parade that was tame to the point of being sedate.

I parked in the Treme, that erstwhile bastion of blackness, raucousness, and of celebratory chaos I fell in love with years ago.

Perhaps it's inappropriate to generalize. I doubt every house in Treme is going for half a million. But the charming Creole cottage I once rented now lists for $495,000, and it abuts a house that should have been condemned back when Clinton was president.

As for the second line that kicked off from the Backstreet Cultural Museum, I won't go as far as the man I overheard saying that there was too much of the "good element" present for it to be authentic, but I will agree with a local documentarian who laughed at what he called the contrived nature of the parade.

Too few booties shook. Nobody dropped it like it was hot. OK, so there was that dude who climbed into the bed of a truck on Barracks Street and danced solo for a few bars. But don't expect to see him in a photographic exhibit of Treme. His dancing fell far short of the spectacular. And Treme, at its finest, is a neighborhood of spectacles.

Take Chief Al, for example. He was wearing a promotional baseball cap from Goodyear, the tire company. He had his khaki pants legs stuffed into his overly long white tube socks, and his black shoes, though fitted, looked suspiciously like a pair of slippers. I stopped him, as he bicycled down St. Claude Avenue, to ask if he wasn't the guy I interviewed the week after the storm, the one who said he wasn't leaving New Orleans no matter what the mayor and the police chief ordered. We had talked about more than Hurricane Katrina that September afternoon. He had volunteered his opinion that some of the young bucks masking as skeletons had become a little too innovative, had incorporated a few too many outside traditions, to suit him.

Sunday, the same Al who had told me he wasn't leaving New Orleans said he was about done with the whole state of Louisiana. He's leaving.

"Now that's the biggest lie told out here today," said a passerby named Frank. Frank asked Al where he'd been. Sick, Al answered, except he didn't say it that way. He said, "Man, I been pronounced dead!"

Really? Frank asked, except he didn't say it that way. He shouted, "Naw, Junior!"

To which Al said, "I didn't even mask Mardi Gras." Frank looked as if he didn't believe it, wouldn't believe it. But there was the proof on Al's arm: a wristband issued by Touro Infirmary—presumably before Mardi Gras.

Soon after that exchange, a white van pulled up in front of the museum, and Wynton Marsalis stepped out. He was to soon premiere his composition "Congo Square" in Congo Square itself, using the second-line parade to make a triumphant entry into Armstrong Park.

While the crowd that had gathered on St. Claude may have expected Marsalis to lead us to Congo Square with the bell of his blaring trumpet pointed skyward, he instead grabbed a cowbell and a taped-up drumstick and joined the percussionists bringing up the rear.

His love for his hometown notwithstanding, it may have been Marsalis' presence that gave the parade an air of contrivance. Many of the city's most famous and accomplished musicians have marched through Treme and blended in to the point of near anonymity, but Marsalis is a world-renowned, Pulitzer-Prize-winning local boy done good. He has star power. So rather than dance with abandon, many people instead focused on getting their picture taken with Marsalis. He graciously obliged them all.

And then we turned from Esplanade Avenue onto Rampart Street, the band broke into "I'll Fly Away," and everybody sang. We were loud and often off-key. We were passing through a neighborhood that may have changed irreversibly but employing our unshakable joie de vivre.

IF WE DIDN'T WEEP, WE WEREN'T HUMAN

MAY 5, 2006

My moment came Sunday morning, Sept. 4. When I walked into the sanctuary at Second Baptist Church in Baton Rouge, the congregation had already begun singing an Andraé Crouch composition taken verbatim from Verse 1 of the 103rd Psalm: "Bless the Lord, O my soul / And all that is within me, bless his holy name."

I had trouble with the second verse of the song, the one that repeats: "He has done great things." First, there was a theological hurdle: How could I sing such a thing after the destruction I'd just seen? Then there was the physical hurdle: How could I sing while sobbing?

Soon after the strongest of the winds died down Aug. 29, I stood on Interstate 10 and looked down on people who had already taken extraordinary measures to keep their heads above the rising water. Three men paddling a boat yelled that they'd just left a house on North Miro Street where 13 people, including some elderly folks and a pregnant woman, were stranded. I don't know if the men realized it, but they, too, appeared to be in danger. There were power lines above their heads, and if the water kept rising, there was the potential they could be electrocuted.

After seeing those men paddling and that woman sitting on her roof and that old man with his arms thrown around an orange water cooler hanging on for life, after asking firefighters about the billows of smoke rising in the distance and hearing them say they'd have to let it burn, after seeing people wander the interstate barefoot and despondent or emerge from attic windows like so many wingless butterflies, I heard myself saying, "OK. My house is probably gone." There may have been resignation in my voice, but if so, that was the only emotion. That was neither the time nor the place to mourn. Nor was it the time to let worry about my house distract me from the important work ahead.

I held the tears at bay for six days. But on the seventh day. . .

That Sunday morning service wasn't the last time I cried. Nor was that cry the most cathartic. Such designation belongs to the weeping I did more than a month later in the parking lot of The Mall at Cortana on Florida Boulevard in Baton Rouge. I was on the phone explaining to a therapist how the loss of some family heirlooms made me a failure as a custodian and how I'd hoped that my mother would validate my guilt by yelling at me. My mother never yells, least of all at me, so there was no chance she'd bring down on me the punishment I thought my failure warranted. And yet, it was the fact that she didn't respond angrily that intensified my guilt and prompted me to reveal my anguish to a therapist.

Mayor Ray Nagin cried, too. We learn this from historian Douglas Brinkley, author of the upcoming book "The Great Deluge: Hurricane Katrina, New Orleans, and the Mississippi Gulf Coast," excerpted in Vanity

Fair magazine. That's hardly remarkable. If Nagin had not wept, one would have to question his humanity.

Had another writer chronicled Nagin's alleged moments of sorrow, frustration, anger and fear, it probably would have come off as the kind of thorough history the public has come to expect. But in a television interview last year, Brinkley heatedly accused Nagin of having blood on his hands. In his written account, Brinkley relies on some of the mayor's political enemies as sources. As a result, his focus on Nagin's private emotional moments seems intended not to flesh him out but to humiliate him.

Perhaps that will play well in Peoria. Maybe Brinkley will find readers so far removed from our situation they'll find it easy to ridicule a weeping man. But here in New Orleans, the man who hasn't wept sticks out, and the man who seeks approval for mocking the tearful would do well to search for another audience.

LINE UP FOR JOY

MAY 19, 2006

I was standing in a line at City Hall Tuesday afternoon between two women discussing their post-Katrina weight gain and a woman heaping hosannas upon a local pastor who took the spot behind her.

The two women ahead of me—one munching popcorn and the other peanut M&Ms—had each gained 26 pounds since the storm, and each professed not to be hungry even as she chewed.

The woman behind me was saying, "You're a blessed man!" as the pastor reached in his suit jacket, removed a white face cloth and patted his face and brow. It wasn't hot. But he was a preacher. The lady addressed him by name, and when he asked hers, she exclaimed, "Blessed and Highly Favored! That's my name, too."

Her use of the word "too" made the preacher think he and she shared the same name, but she corrected him. "Blessed and Highly Favored" is her name, she said.

He wiped his face. A prolonged wipe.

The time was 12:50 p.m., and the five of us were lined up outside door 1W37 to pay or challenge bills we'd received for city services. Alpat, a Slidell collection agency, had sent me notice that the $13 I owed the city for a past-due sanitation bill had been turned over for collection. What past-due sanitation bill?

A sign said the office closes for the lunch hour, and when the door opened at 12:55, the women ahead of me perked up. But the man who opened the door was going for a smoke. "You don't need to be smoking them cigarettes," Madame Popcorn said, and as the man continued his walk toward the exit, she and M&Ms suspended their conversation about their overeating to agree how bad it is to smoke. Meanwhile, B.A.H.F. was talking to the pastor about other pastors they both knew, and he was telling her how much her praise had brightened his day.

At 1 p.m., the door opened, and we spilled into the office. The preacher and M&Ms were redirected to an adjacent office where their specific issues could be addressed, leaving behind me, Madame Popcorn, B.A.H.F. and the woman behind the desk.

B.A.H.F, who, as it turns out, goes by a different name for billing purposes, told the woman behind the desk that the preacher is one of the most important men in the city, implying that she hadn't shown him proper deference when she sent him away. The woman behind the desk simulated a walking motion with the fingers closest to her thumb and said, "He got two legs," to which Madame Popcorn nodded in agreement. "I respect 'em," the woman behind the desk said of preachers in general, but her tone made it clear that she wasn't gonna throw down palm branches in their path.

There were a few seconds of silence as checks were scribbled out and affidavits were signed. Then B.A.H.F. said, "How you doing, young man?"

I said, "I'm doing well. Thank you." She worries about young black men and prays we're going to be all right. Then suddenly: "You love the Lord?"

I said, "Yes, ma'am." To the woman behind the desk she squealed, "Oooooooh, he said yes! Gimme a hug!" She handed me what looked to be a dollar but was instead a religious tract.

A woman who took the second desk told me that the $13 was billed Aug. 26. So how come I wasn't asked to pay it before it was sent to collections? I wouldn't have been around to receive the bill, she said. Did I want to write a check? Why hadn't I brought my checkbook?

I'd assumed it was an error, is why. I had $12 and something that looked like a dollar but wasn't. I mentioned the nearby ATM. "I don't want you to have to pay two-fifty for a dollar," she said, referring to the fee the machine exacts, and she pulled from her purse the extra buck I needed. Now who's blessed and highly favored?

B.A.H.F. herself had already left, but I wish I could have thanked her and the others for giving me another answer to the question, "What do you like about New Orleans?" The answer is the people, who can make an ordinary bill-paying trip a joy.

THUGS TAKE A HACKSAW TO OUR SPIRIT

DECEMBER 29, 2006

Art, by its very nature, is worth more than the ingredients that give it shape. A clay pot is worth more than the lump of clay from which it was formed, a painting more than the paint and canvas. Similarly, the bronze sculptures in John Scott's eastern New Orleans studio were worth more than the bronze itself.

But to the thieves who used a bolt cutter, hacksaw and a hammer to dismantle Scott's exceptional sculptures, his pieces were worth no more than their composite parts, worth no more than the going rate at the neighborhood scrap metal emporium.

The ransacking of the studio that Scott shared with artist Ron Bechet would be slightly less infuriating if we could believe the thieves knew what they were stealing—or if they'd been content just to steal. A heist—similar to the 2004 robbery that removed Edvard Munch's paintings "The Scream" and "Madonna" from the Munch Museum in Oslo—would have been understandable, if no less criminal. Since Norway police recovered those paintings in August, museum officials have discovered moisture and abrasion damage. Even so, we can be assured that the masked gunmen who lifted the paintings from the walls of the museum knew what they were taking.

Not so our thieves. Their decision to hammer, cut and hack at Scott's art is convincing evidence that they had no idea of its value. The art was the pearls. They were the swine trampling it.

There would be no good time—absolutely none—for an artist to have his life's work violated. Even so, it's hard to imagine that this crime could have come at a worse time for Scott. Exiled to Houston by Hurricane Katrina, a pulmonary fibrosis diagnosis has forced him to have two lung transplants. The first pair of lungs didn't function.

In January, before he had had either operation, he spoke to columnist Lolis Eric Elie between coughs. Yes, his studio had flooded, but his paper and canvas works were mostly on the second floor. As for the first floor, the pieces there were made out of metal. They could be cleaned.

Bechet discovered the break-in Tuesday when he dropped by the studio with plans to check on things and do a little cleaning. He saw that his paintings had been scattered, that his friend's sculptures were gone. As he told reporter Doug MacCash, "All I could do was scream. I was so angry I could feel the blood in my head. I had to sit down for a while."

To think that Scott's works will now be valued solely on their weight—that they'll be tossed onto a heap with air conditioning units, mufflers, copper gutters and telephone wires—should prompt everybody who loves this city and everybody who has even the slightest appreciation of art to scream. What has this city become?

I haven't seen as much of John Scott's work as I should have. But the piece of his I saw in April 2001 I'll never forget. It's a metal sculpture of Birmingham's 16th

Street Baptist Church on Sept. 15, 1963. It appears at first sight that there are plumes of smoke rising from the building. But then one sees that what first appears to be smoke are the spirits of four little girls—killed by KKK dynamite—and rising heavenward.

I don't know if that piece was pilfered too (or if it was even at the studio), but I do know that if it was, it could fetch two or three bucks easy.

"John's in the hospital, this place is a wreck, and now people are trying to take stuff," Bechet said. "I'm not sure how good this will be for his morale."

I'm not sure how good it will be for any of ours.

BLAST FROM THE PAST

The 1927 explosion that flooded St. Bernard Parish echoed in rumors of sabotage during Betsy and Katrina

APRIL 29, 2007

A levee can really take the worry off a person's mind. Well, to an extent. Levees can break. And where they break—this side of the river or the other, this parish or the next one—can mean the difference between life and death, between prosperity and destitution. That's why one would worry about sabotage, why at a certain point in our history, men patrolled their levees with firearms. It was an article of faith that during times of high water, levees were prone to attack, especially at night, and needed to be guarded.

What happened 80 years ago served as proof that stealth isn't required to destroy a levee. One might argue that it proved the impossibility of stealthily destroying some levees.

On April 29, 1927, the Mississippi River levee at Caernarvon was dynamited on the orders of a group of New Orleanians calling themselves the Citizens Flood Relief Committee. Flood Causing Committee would have been more accurate because it was that group that decided that—contrary to river stage predictions—the Mississippi needed to be let loose on St. Bernard Parish.

The committee and the elected officials who did its bidding argued that flooding St. Bernard would spare New Orleans from flooding. But New Orleans was going to be spared anyway because levees way upriver were known to be much too weak to resist the swollen river.

Author John Barry in "Rising Tide," the definitive book about the Great Flood of 1927, suggests that the committee was more concerned with showing financiers in New York that it would always be safe to invest in New Orleans, that the city controlled the river and not the other way round. Even as the levee was being dynamited, Barry writes, a publicity committee was preparing to distribute the good news to 2,100 banks and businesses around the country. Not that they wouldn't have found out. The scene was lousy with reporters, photographers and onlookers.

The dynamite charges the Orleans Levee Board set off on April 29, 1927, destroyed more than the levee at Caernarvon. If there were any poor people who believed in egalitarianism, the dynamite destroyed that, too. It validated every conspiracy theory that accused the rich of playing god with the lives of the poor.

Thirty-eight years later, when Hurricane Betsy swamped the Lower 9th Ward, rumors circulated that the strategy to sacrifice poor neighborhoods for wealthier ones had been stealthily employed this time. Forty years after Betsy, when the same neighborhood was hit with a virtual tsunami, people like Andrew Baker of Tennessee Street gave voice to a common suspicion: "God didn't play a part in this. They always do that. They flood the Lower 9."

There's no evidence to support the claims that the Industrial Canal levee was purposely destroyed to flood the Lower 9th Ward, but who can blame poor black folks for assuming that they would be treated at least as poorly as poor white folks in St. Bernard had been treated? In what universe do poor black people catch a break?

It's a question that can only be addressed with a question. If the oligarchy in New Orleans trumpeted its decision to blow up St. Bernard's levees, and The Times-Picayune (neither a passive nor objective observer) futilely chided readers not to bring picnic baskets to the demolition, why would that same power structure have kept secret a plan to destroy black people's property? In what universe do rich white people fear the wrath of poor black folks?

While 1927 demonstrated how far the elite were willing to go to protect their stuff, it's important to point out that their plan was not easily executed. Despite their careful orchestration and the cooperation of the military, it took repeated applications of dynamite before the levee completely gave way. All in all demolition took at least 60 laborers, 10 days and 39 tons of dynamite.

Still, the idea persists that a few people can destroy a levee quickly, stealthily, in hurricane conditions without leaving behind evidence. Those inclined to believe that would probably say the technology of explosives has come a long way since 1927. They'd be right.

But the idea that 9th Ward floodwalls have been sabotaged isn't rooted in an understanding of explosives. Rather, it's rooted in the historical knowledge that levees make enticing targets and in the well-founded belief that, to the strong, the lives of the weak are dispensable.

DIGNITY EXPOSED TO THE ELEMENTS

MAY 6, 2007

"Dishonours which better fit our enemies are now
being piled up on the ones we love."
                                    – "Antigone," Sophocles

*   *   *

One notices that certain New Orleanians talking about
recently deceased loved ones focus more on the inter-
ment than the death itself. "We buried my mama on
Saturday" is a more common way of expressing one's
loss than "My mama died on Tuesday."

Perhaps the emphasis is on burying because that verb
demonstrates that the survivors did something tangible to honor the beloved. Dust returns to dust, and
no body's exempt, but in burying our loved ones, we
guarantee that the decomposition proceeds in a digni-
fied manner—in a way that doesn't assault our sense of
sight or sense of smell.

Leaving a body outside to publicly decompose was
considered an indignity when Sophocles wrote "Anti-
gone" in 442 B.C., which is why the title character is determined to defy the state and give her brother a proper
burial.

Leaving a body exposed was no less an indignity the beginning of September 2005 when the state—in the form of its military—forced Herbert Freeman Jr. to leave his mother's body in the heat and humidity of New Orleans. Ethel Mayo Freeman, 91, died in front of the Ernest N. Morial Convention Center waiting for federal officials to rescue her.

Times-Picayune photographer Ted Jackson documented the elderly woman's body, slumped in a wheelchair and covered with a blanket. There were many images of suffering that came out of New Orleans that week, but I'm not sure that any other more poignantly conveyed the consequences of the federal government's foot-dragging.

The U.S. Army Corps of Engineers' levees broke Monday morning. Ethel Freeman, after calling out for medical attention, died Thursday. Who among us wants to argue that the United States of America, the most powerful nation on the planet, could not have reached Mrs. Freeman before she died? What good is power if it isn't used beneficently?

When the soldiers finally did arrive three days later and said they'd only be transporting the living, Herbert Freeman requested a private moment. Before he boarded the bus, couldn't he have just a minute to push his mother's body into a more secluded place, a place where she'd be out of the elements and folks couldn't gawk at her?

His request was denied. He was only given enough time to write a note with her name and his and his cell phone number. He left the note with the body.

The son's anger must have been intense before the soldiers arrived. But to be denied the opportunity to show his respect must have magnified it further.

Last year Herbert Freeman sued the United States government and its bureaucrats for wrongful death, claiming that but for their negligence his mother would not have died. Shortly thereafter he told Newsday, "I'm still looking to regain her dignity and respect that she lost on the streets of New Orleans."

U.S. District Court Judge Jay Zainey expressed sympathy for Freeman's loss and acknowledged that the federal government by its own admission made mistakes. But in dismissing the wrongful death claim, Judge Zainey wrote, "One can only speculate at this point whether those mistakes caused the tragic deaths of the decedents."

As sorry as he feels for Herbert Freeman, Judge Zainey wrote, the law just isn't on his side, and as a judge, he can't award him money.

I know Freeman sought monetary damages in his lawsuit, but in reading his quotes and watching him on screen, I've never been convinced that money is his aim. His mother, an American citizen, was dishonored. And a loving son just can't abide that.

WORKING TOO HARD TO BEG FOLKS TO STAY

JULY 20, 2007

The last time we spoke she promised she'd appear when she sensed New Orleans needed her.

"What are you?" I asked Bea Rill. "Some kind of fairy godmother-slash-Batman, some kind of homespun genie who'll appear and crack wise after three quick rubs on a gumbo pot?"

She seemed to take offense at my disrespect, became uncharacteristically sober and said, "No, baby, I'm that character who appears when I feel to believe you're too afraid to say it."

"Say what?"

"Whatever needs to be said," she said, and with that she was gone.

I interpreted her promise to mean she'd only pop her head up for the big things. It surprised me, then, that she emerged to complain about something as small as a Times-Picayune letter to the editor.

After inquiring about my mama'n'em and my house and my Road Home status, she said, "Listen, y'all got a policy against alter egos responding to letters?"

"It would probably raise some eyebrows," I said. "Why? What's got you worked up?"

"The complainers," she said, "the excuse makers, the ones who want us to take our hands off the plow so we might pat them on the back for being here."

"The doctor?" I said. "Who went to some fancy school? That the letter you're talking about?"

"Well, yeah," she said, "but had it been just one letter writer, I could've let that slide. A random guy who's frustrated? Whatever. But he isn't the first one, and though there's probably nothing I can say to make him the last one, I got to say something. That whole mindset's got my pressure up."

"You might want to see a doctor about that pressure," I said. "As for the other part, what mindset exactly?"

"The it-needs-to-be-easier-here-cuz-I'm-here mindset, the I-could-have-been-somewhere-else mindset. The somebody-notice-me-leaving-and-beg-me-pretty-please-to-stay kind of foolishness."

I could tell she was angry. She took a breath. I heard her exhale. "Listen, it's hard here. Lord knows it is. There are days when I get my Entergy bill or my water bill, and I wonder if this month is gonna be the month when ole Bea Rill has a breakdown. Some days driving home from work, I just want to scream, 'To hell with it all!' This city and this state, these politicians and these politicians' defenders and my insurance company and these murderers and these crooked cops and to anybody making it hard on folks, ordinary folks, trying to live here."

I wanted to say something—I really did—but everything I thought of sounded trite. So I didn't say anything.

"There's like this New Orleans tax, you know? You've got to pay more money right off the bat to live here.

Rent, utilities, tire repair, insurance. Then you got to worry about the different ways you could be killed—from drowning to stroking out to gunfire.

"But you know something? Crazy as it may be, I choose to be here. That doctor act like he the only one in New Orleans got options. Shoot, he ain't the only one."

"You've thought about leaving?"

"Oooh, yes indeed. My skills are transferable. You've got to remember, baby, I'm the answer lady, the information connoisseur. You think I couldn't find a way to make it in Memphis or Kansas City or Kalamazoo? Of course, I wouldn't make as much as a physician, but that's no requirement because I never have."

"But you yourself admit that it's hard here. I think that's the point of some of these complaints."

"And my point is that it's hard on everybody: from the Ph.Ds. to the no-degrees. But this is an all-volunteer army. There is no draft, and there's no penalty for walking off the battlefield.

"But if you do leave, do us all a favor and just go. We've got no time to wave, let alone wring our hands. We've got a whole lot more rebuilding to do."

INJUSTICE IN JENA

SEPTEMBER 23, 2007

A noose is an implement of death.

It is not a toy. It is not a prop for a practical joke. It is a knot of oppression, a neck-strangling tool of old-fashioned American terrorism. A noose can kill, and even when it doesn't, it antagonizes.

Forget its former use in procedurally correct, state-sponsored executions; for black Americans, the noose is emblematic of an absence of justice. It is what black criminals got instead of due process and a reminder of a time when a black person didn't even have to break the law to meet the rope.

It was in that spirit—punishment for no discernible offense—that nooses were brought out at Jena High School in LaSalle Parish. Black students were granted "permission" by the principal to sit under an oak tree that tradition held was for white students. The principal told the black students they could sit anywhere, but their integration attempt prompted the aggrieved to hang three nooses from the tree.

The principal recommended expulsion for three students he deemed responsible for the nooses, but the school board overruled him and returned the offenders to school. No students of history, they, the members of the LaSalle Parish School Board, chose to see the incident as a harmless prank and not as a hostile act promising violence.

Is it a surprise that some of the students in Jena are so backward when such are the adults in charge of their education?

Nooses are, of course, symbolic of a history of injustice, but the ones on that tree served as omens of injustice yet to come. Both black and white students fought in Jena, but the black students' actions were the ones the district attorney abhors.

At an off-campus party designated whites only, a black student audacious enough to appear was attacked. According to some reports, he had a bottle broken over his head. His attacker was charged with simple battery and sentenced to probation.

Days later, a young white man said to have been among the attackers at the party was accused of threatening the victim and two other black students with a sawed-off shotgun. They overpowered him and took the gun to police, who arrested them for stealing it.

Three nooses, a bottle and a sawed-off shotgun: Those were the weapons white Jena students used to threaten or attack their black victims. Six black students, including the one beaten at the party and menaced with the shotgun, used their feet to fight back. They stomped one of the white students they believed to be behind the nooses and the attacks.

Their victim reportedly lost consciousness during the attack but recovered quickly. The district attorney, who assures us he isn't racist, originally charged the six with attempted murder and conspiracy to commit murder. Their rubber-bottomed tennis shoes, he argued, were deadly weapons. The six students later had their charges reduced to aggravated battery and conspiracy to commit aggravated battery.

Tens of thousands of people marched on Jena Thursday to highlight the injustice, but despite their efforts, one defendant remains locked up, and others are still scheduled for trial.

One wishes those black students hadn't responded violently, if only because the system is rigged against them. The message of the noose is that black-on-white attacks are considered an order of magnitude worse than the other way around.

Remember that scene in John Grisham's "A Time To Kill"? The white defense attorney had to convince an all-white jury that a black man had the right to murder the white men who raped his little girl. But he didn't win the jurors over with the facts. He won them over when he asked them to imagine what they'd do if their daughter was raped—by black men. That scene works as fiction because oftentimes in real life the blackness of a perpetrator is deemed an aggravating factor.

Only the hopelessly naive would argue that such thinking is relegated to the past. It's certainly not in the past in LaSalle Parish—although maybe the all-white jury wouldn't have convicted Mychal Bell of aggravated battery if the defendant's black public defender had bestirred himself to present a defense.

But that black lawyer's ineptitude aside, the prosecutor should never have charged Bell and others with serious felonies if he wasn't going to be just as serious about the crimes their white attackers committed against them.

Black people never expected the noose to be applied fairly, but the criminal justice system in 2007? It's supposed to be different.

WHO'S DISTURBING THE PEACE IN TREME?

OCTOBER 9, 2007

The moon inspires awe the whole world over. But that Friday night in March 2001 the moon seemed special-made for New Orleans, a heavenly body emerging from the clouds to bounce light off the rain-slick streets of Treme.

I was in turmoil. I loved a woman who didn't love my city. She lived in one of those just-so places: a gleaming, prosperous city that gets mentioned whenever talk turns to Southern success stories. I lived in New Orleans, where the old is preferred over the new, and the culture thrives without corporate sponsorship.

We were to talk that night. We were scheduled to have one of those futile late-night conversations couples feel obliged to have even after an irreconcilable difference has been discovered.

It was while waiting for her call that I heard the sound of a trumpet. It was after going outside to investigate that I realized the storm was over and saw the moon emerging. It was while standing there watching and listening that I knew I wouldn't be leaving New Orleans any time soon.

Had the crowd of people following the trumpeter down the center of Treme Street secured a parading permit? No more than you'd secure a permit to send a card to a bereaved friend or express your sorrow with a phone call. For that is what that rendition of "I'll Fly Away" was: a communal expression of sympathy that was obviously sincere because it was spontaneous.

One of my neighbors had passed away, and the people in the neighborhood gathered around her house to speak well of her and to speak well of other people in the neighborhood who passed away before she did.

Last week, in that same neighborhood—geographically, at least—two musicians playing "I'll Fly Away" were charged with disturbing the peace. The two were part of a larger group playing in memory of a deceased neighborhood musician, and the group was part of a larger second-line procession. However, somebody in the neighborhood considered the whole thing a racket and reported the mourners to police.

I spent enough time in Treme to know that the bands that parade through can be loud. But the memory that sticks out the most for me is that beautiful, moonlit, rain-soaked night. That trumpet solo didn't disturb the peace. If anything, it helped create a peacefulness that everybody standing outside could feel.

New Orleans Police Superintendent Warren Riley on Monday afternoon decried a culture that avoids placing a simple phone call to the police to let the department know an escort will be needed for a second-line planned that night.

Maybe it is as simple as the police chief says. But his statement implies that the "organizers" of a given neighborhood memorial know Monday afternoon that they're going to be staging a second line Monday night. It implies advance planning where it so seldom exists.

Standing on a stoop on Treme Street, I once saw a parade for a homeless man. The word on the street was that it was a spur-of-the-moment parade. A man everybody knew had died, so everybody he knew jumped into the street and danced for him.

It just doesn't seem right, the expectation that the folks in Treme go ask permission to send off the people they love, go ask the folks in power to let them celebrate the lives of those who helped form the fabric of the neighborhood.

The culture that kept me and so many others in New Orleans has thrived without the blessing of the establishment. It has also thrived without the assistance of city officials, the police department in particular.

If somebody is blowing a horn in Treme and somebody else is calling the police, only one of those people is disturbing the peace, and it isn't the one playing music.

87-YEAR-OLD WON'T SEE HOME FINISHED

DECEMBER 16, 2007

It's not hard to figure out the kind of man Vernon Washington Sr. was. He was 87 years old and, along with a volunteer group from Tennessee, was helping rebuild 1209 Charbonnet St. in the Lower 9th Ward.

The Charbonnet house didn't belong to Washington but to his deceased brother. Even so, the old man meant to live there. His own house, over on North Johnson Street, had been destroyed, like thousands of other ones, on Aug. 29, 2005. He had had to hack a hole in the roof to escape the rising water. He had had to wait—three days, his son says—for help to arrive. And then he had been evacuated to a hospital where he was treated for dehydration.

But Washington—who had worked as a longshoreman, an iceman, a floor finisher and in other construction trades—came back to New Orleans. He lived in one FEMA trailer and then another. And then it came time to take the FEMA trailers away.

Tony Sferlazza, a carpenter with the volunteer group Plenty International, said after FEMA employees came and took Washington's FEMA trailer away, the agency set him up in a hotel room in the city. And, Sferlazza said, that's where Washington spent Wednesday night, Dec. 5.

Plenty International helps build houses at cost, Sferlazza said. All the labor is donated. The house was almost done, he said. They needed the city's inspectors to come out and examine their work before the utilities could be turned on.

As for Washington checking into the hotel, there was a momentary hitch that had something to do with whether he had a FEMA identification number. But that had been resolved, Sferlazza said. Washington spent Wednesday night in the hotel, and Sferlazza assumed he'd also spend Thursday night there.

But when Sferlazza arrived at the house on Charbonnet Street Friday, Dec. 7, he realized that Washington had made the fatal decision to spend Thursday night there.

Sferlazza said he found Washington's body on "a bare mattress. No blanket. No pillow. He was cold."

"The inspectors came while I was waiting for the coroner," Sferlazza said. That means, he said, that the house could have been powered up as soon as Monday or Tuesday.

Local FEMA spokesman Bob Josephson said Friday that Washington was the last person to leave the group trailer site the agency established on St. Claude Avenue. He was offered a hotel room, Josephson said, but Washington said he was really close to finishing his house and could go there.

Washington's family didn't know he'd decided to sleep in the cold house. They didn't even know he was no longer in the FEMA trailer, his son Vernon Washington Jr. said. "I didn't find that out until after it happened," he said.

The younger Washington, who lives in California, said he had talked to his father a few days earlier about the progress being made on the house on Charbonnet Street. "At that point he told me they only had a couple more days" of work to do, he said.

"He was extremely hard-working," the son said of his father, "and he believed in getting things done right, without any shortcuts."

That Vernon Washington Sr. was a hard worker goes without saying, considering that he was 87 and putting all his energy into rebuilding a home in the neighborhood he loved. Even so, Sferlazza said that during one of his last conversations with Washington, the old man thanked him for all the help he and his group had provided.

"He said, 'Son, when this job is over I'm gonna hang up my tools.'"

Somebody else will have to hang them up for him. Vernon Washington Sr. died before he could finish.

THE ROAD HOME THINKS YOU'RE ON CRACK

MARCH 7, 2008

There are myriad big-ticket items I could buy: a Cadillac Escalade, a high-definition television with top-of-the-line surround-sound speakers, courtside season tickets for the Hornets, 20-inch rims that spin unnecessarily.

Then again, some are betting that I'll blow my money on crack. It would take longer to lose it all that way, but I suppose it could be done.

Boring as it may sound, though, I think I'm going to use the proceeds from the sale of my house to the Road Home to buy yet another house. Road Home money comes with plenty aggravation. So I'll assume that other Louisianans who applied to get it will use it for housing, too. They'll either repair their old homes or buy new ones. After all, crack doesn't keep the chill off.

Why is it necessary to defend my intentions? Or the intentions of others like me who did nothing more than have their houses flooded by the Army Corps of Engineers?

Because of Tom.

Because of Kathleen Blanco.

Tom was the unfailingly pleasant attorney who walked me through my first Road Home closing. You might remember my first Road Home closing. That was when the state tried to give me $97,000 more than the amount we'd agreed upon. So my first concern wasn't Tom but how to give the money back.

I didn't ask Tom for any of his opinions. Still, the self-professed admirer of Ann Coulter volunteered them. People aren't going to do right, he said. Three years from closing, when the state asks recipients for evidence of home repairs, they're going to be in a pickle because they won't have made any.

Tom also passed along a prediction he said came from a captain in the New Orleans Police Department: that all this Road Home money hitting the streets is going to start a "crack war." He envisioned grandchildren strong-arming grandmothers for the money and using it for evil.

Because later that day I was scheduled to speak at Ochsner Medical Center's annual Martin Luther King Jr. program, I showed up at the grant closing wearing a suit and tie. Perhaps Tom felt comfortable sharing news of the impending crack war because I didn't look like I'd be fighting in it.

He asked me what I did for a living, and I told him. He'd always thought he'd make a good columnist, he said. He then helpfully suggested that I write about my experience at my Road Home closing. I told him maybe I would.

To be fair, Tom wasn't scornful of all Road Home's travelers. As he explained, "most" of the people showing up for closings are homeowners. Most? How about that?

Though Tom expressed his opinions a little more bluntly and was more extreme than our former governor, the suspicions he expressed for the people showing up to close their grants didn't sound much different from the ones she expressed.

There was a time when I was willing to give Blanco the benefit of the doubt, when I was open to the idea that, notwithstanding the program's policies, she wasn't personally skeptical of Road Home applicants.

But then she defended those condescending policies by explaining to me that a Road Home disbursement could be the first big check some people ever received. She didn't want them blowing their money on something other than housing.

Never mind the fact that all—not most, Tom—of the program's applicants are homeowners and that homeowners tend toward the financially responsible. All would still be treated as potential fraud cases and be talked down to by the state.

Apparently, all Blanco's fretting was for naught. To hear Tom tell it, all the wrong people still got in and still made it all the way through the program. Who knows what they're going to do with their windfall?

If I had to guess, I'd say they're going to use the money to repair, buy or build a house. Forgive me if I assume most recipients will be honest. I just don't see any reason why folks who were unfairly flooded ought to have their character assailed.

AT BETHUNE, RX FOR EXCELLENCE

OCTOBER 18, 2009

Principal Mary Haynes-Smith talks about the students at Mary McLeod Bethune Elementary the way a doctor would talk about patients. She diagnoses their concerns early—even before they could rightly be called problems—and the solutions she and her staff come up with, she calls "prescriptions."

Take, for example, the Integrated Louisiana Educational Assessment Program, the so-called iLEAP, that's given to Haynes-Smith's third graders. Students who score basic—that is, those who pass the test but don't impress—get a prescription from the principal that includes a summer in the classroom with "extra doses of reading and math." There, at summer school, they get more attention from teachers than they would get during the school year. The student-teacher ratio there is 6:1, Haynes-Smith said.

"We know our kids' weaknesses early and their strengths early," she said. "We knew all our kids passed" the iLEAP, she said, "but some were just basic or approaching basic." And to her, that's not good enough. "We would love them to score mastery," she said.

That early intervention surely explains why every fourth grader at the Hollygrove school passed the iLEAP this spring. To pass the high-stakes test, students must score basic in either English or math and score approaching basic in the other subject. Every one of Haynes-Smith's fourth graders passed the English portion, with 79 percent of them achieving mastery and 14 percent testing as advanced. Only 96 percent of her fourth-graders scored basic or above in math, but because the two students who scored approaching basic in math had scored at least basic in English, they were promoted to fifth grade.

Last week, state education officials released school performance scores for campuses around the state, and Mary McLeod Bethune Elementary School of Literature and Technology was typically impressive. The school, which educates students between pre-kindergarten and sixth grade and is one of the few campuses under the control of the Orleans Parish School Board, had a 2007-08 baseline school performance score of 107.8. It reached its growth target this year with a school performance score of 125.2. To meet next year's growth target, the school has to get better still.

New Orleans is a divided city. On the one hand, there are people who can't even imagine a traditional school—especially not one run by the school board—turning out scholars. On the other hand, there are traditionalists who refuse to classify charter schools as public and who oppose them partly because teacher unions aren't welcome there. Bethune is an old-school school in a poor neighborhood—Haynes-Smith said more than 99 percent of her students qualify for free or reduced lunch—that got almost the exact same score (125.2) as St. Tammany Parish's Madisonville Elementary School (125.5).

Yes, the school's achievements challenge the age-old assumption that nothing good can come out of the Orleans Parish School Board and the more recent belief that a school has to adopt a new management structure to succeed. But that's not the most important message—at least not in my book. Bethune is educating children whom some would presume ineducable. The principal at every school—charter, recovery, school board or otherwise—needs to adopt the attitude that Bethune's principal has: that basic isn't good enough, that mastery is to be pursued.

When I spoke with Haynes-Smith on the phone Friday morning, it was clear that she's proud of what she's been able to accomplish as an administrator but that she's prouder still at where she's been able to be successful: Hollygrove.

"It feels so good," she said, knowing that she's taken students who have so little and given them so much. "The greatest reward," she said, comes "from students with the greatest need."

The chasm between the haves and the have-nots has never been small in this country, but it seems much more significant now that so much instruction requires technology. Students at Bethune all get laptop computers, Haynes-Smith said. Perhaps as important, parents are included in the school's technology training. That helps give parents—who may have never owned a computer before—a basic facility with the machines and allows the students and their parents to "talk the same language," she said.

But technological innovation can't get all the credit for the school's success. The staff works hard to shape their students' character, the principal told me. With good behavior and good grades, boys at the school are included in a club called "Distinguished Gentlemen." They are provided with blazers, shirts and ties. Their female counterparts are in a club called "Ladies of Destiny." It's there that they learn "how they can help each other and keep each other out of trouble," Haynes-Smith said.

Speaking of destiny, it was when Haynes-Smith was around the age of those young girls that she resolved to create a new school environment.

She was "petrified" of one of her elementary school teachers, and her assessment that the woman was mean hasn't changed over time. Bethune's future principal vowed to teach herself because even as a child she knew "that's not how you treat children."

EMPTINESS DWELLS WHERE HOME ONCE STOOD

JANUARY 29, 2010

> "You know, looked like 10,000 people were stand-
> ing 'round the buryin' ground. / I didn't know I
> loved her till they let her down."
> >   —Son House, "Death Letter Blues"

*   *   *

They knocked down my house Saturday. My first house, my only house, the three-bedroom purchase that symbolized for me my transition from quasi-adult to the real thing. Saturday, they knocked it down.

I had received word that the demolition of 1498 Crescent St. was imminent, but when I got there Saturday, the heavy work had been completed. A huge metal bin sat where my house had stood, and the broken-up blue bits of the house filled the bin to its rim.

Men in hard hats milled about. Did they know that the last occupant of the house had pulled up and was watching them work? Would they have done anything different if they had known? Shaken my hand, shrugged their shoulders, muttered a quick "sorry" and averted their eyes? There was no need to test it. I stayed in my car and drove away after a few silent moments of observation.

I never seriously considered going back after Katrina. I had only lived there 18 months. Not long enough to form a strong sentimental attachment but more than enough time to experience the headaches. Just weeks after I bought the house, my insurance company dumped me. Your roof has two layers, they said. The home inspector had noted that on his paperwork but had not told me, a first-time buyer, that it was a problem. It was. A new insurance company, a significantly higher monthly payment, and I hadn't even moved in.

Cracks began to appear in the walls. As the ground continued to sink and the house shifted with it, the side door became harder to shut and keep shut. More than once, my neighbors closed it after finding that it had popped open while I was away.

Even before Katrina, the house had problems from top to bottom. Why go back if I could avoid it?

It felt strange—almost shameful—to have lost a house to the broken levees and feel halfway relieved about it. Then came the anger of being denied the anticipated full feeling of relief. I was no longer living in a house with a bad roof and a sinking foundation, but thanks to the Road Home program's dawdling, I had to keep making mortgage and insurance payments through February 2008. And pay for rent on top of that.

When I finally signed the house over to the state of Louisiana, I felt liberated. So why the sadness Saturday when I saw that the house I'd owned had been taken down? Why the sudden flood of sentimentality and nostalgia? Had I been fonder of the house than I'd let on, even to myself?

That's probably part of it. But more significant than that is the feeling that part of my personal history has been erased. Again.

Except for the couple snapshots I've found at my parents' house, I don't have pictures of me as a college student. My diploma was destroyed in the flood, too. I doubt I'll ever forget my four years at Washington University, but how I'd love to have photographs to point to. I received a good education, but I still miss the sight of a framed diploma on the wall.

In the same way, I know I owned a house. I shared a Thanksgiving meal there with my family. I hosted a graduation party when my sister finished Dillard, and I remember the hilarious attempts by my dad and uncles to fix my new gas grill. It was so hard to fix because it wasn't broken.

Even though I didn't live there anymore—even though I thought going back would be more trouble than it was worth—the house remained a stop on my personal disaster tour. I would stop there on the long, winding trip from the 17th Street Canal in Lakeview to the Industrial Canal in the 9th Ward. At those two canals I'd talk about how much the city had lost. At my house I'd talk about how much I had.

It's gone now, and I understand as well as anybody that its demolition is a tangible sign of progress for New Orleans. But it's hard to look at such emptiness and not feel a corresponding emptiness inside.

CAN'T BOTHER TO READ A REPORT? REALLY?

FEBRUARY 28, 2010

Warren Riley was not yet the New Orleans police superintendent when officers—according to a retired lieutenant's guilty plea—went on an unprovoked rampage against pedestrians on the Danziger Bridge. However, it was his responsibility—more than that, it was his promise—as the next police chief to find out what happened on the bridge the Sunday after Hurricane Katrina, to find out if there was anything to the allegations of police officers going berserk.

His promise was printed in this newspaper as a letter to the editor Sept. 24, 2006, after this column criticized what even then appeared to be a police department cover-up of Danziger. He wrote, in part, "While columnists...may have the limitless prerogative to judge complicated criminal and legal matters before they are fully investigated, the fact is that police departments do not. This is why I have not and will not comment on the Danziger Bridge shooting incident while the investigation I began remains in progress. I believe the public understands."

Please note that Riley said he'd begun an investigation. Later, in that same letter, he promises, "There will be no cover-up of the facts in this or any other case we investigate." His goal is to boost the public confidence in the police department, he says, and he will fully disclose the results of his investigation and punish any officer who needs to be punished.

On Thursday Riley said he never read his department's report on the Danziger Bridge shootings.

Two people were killed, one of whom was developmentally disabled. A woman had part of her arm blown off, and her husband was shot in the head. That couple's daughter and nephew were also wounded. A suspect was booked with trying to kill seven police officers and a civilian. Officers were being accused of unleashing a massacre. Later, seven of them were indicted in state court on murder charges. The department's top police officer never read the report? Really?

"I was briefed," he said Thursday. Nothing in that briefing made him think there had been a cover-up, he said. Was that the extent of Riley's vaunted investigation: listening to a summary and not raising an eyebrow?

Admittedly, the chief is trapped between the devil and the deep blue sea. If he says he read the report, he'll be asked why an officer of his standing didn't see it for the implausible work of fiction it was. By saying he didn't read it, though, he's pleading indifference. New Orleanians are dead and disfigured, his officers are accused of criminally attacking them, and he can't be bothered to even flip through the pages of a report.

The officers rushed to Danziger Bridge that Sunday afternoon in a Budget rental truck, responding to a false report that other officers had been shot. They saw pedestrians on the bridge. They shot them.

Michael Lohman, who retired as a lieutenant earlier this month, said Wednesday in federal court that the pedestrians did nothing to provoke the officers. None was carrying a weapon, Lohman said. Even so, as a supervisor on the scene, he went along with a plan to plant a Colt .357 Magnum and accuse pedestrian Lance Madison of having fired it at officers. Lohman says he later saw a police report that was so unbelievable in its description of events that he wrote his own fictional account to replace it. According to court records, even Lohman's report was switched out by another officer who thought it would be better if the cover-up story sounded more like the audio statements officers provided after the shootings.

The day after Lohman's confession, Riley held his press conference. "Today is a dark and disappointing day for the citizens of New Orleans," he said.

The disappointments began well before last week, and they include a police chief prickly enough to fire off a letter to a newspaper but too derelict in his duties to stand up for innocents being slaughtered by his own.

"What I can say is that Michael Lohman deserves to go to jail," Riley said.

There is no criminal charge for police chiefs who choose to see no evil and hear no evil when their cops are accused of murder. If there were, Warren Riley would be in a jail of his own.

FOR BLACK HOMEOWNERS, HOLLOW VICTORY

AUGUST 20, 2010

Moral victories stink.

That's what five black New Orleans homeowners discovered this week when a federal judge in Washington ruled that Louisiana's Road Home Program did indeed give them less money than they'd have received had their houses been destroyed in a white neighborhood—but that he couldn't do anything about it.

The plaintiffs' lawyers say they'll appeal U.S. District Judge Henry Kennedy's position that he's powerless to grant them relief, but as it stands now, Gloria Burns, Rhonda Dents, Almarie Ford, Daphne Jones and Edward Randolph derive no benefits at all from getting a judge to see it their way.

No matter. State officials are still planning to appeal Kennedy's finding and his order that the state use a different formula to calculate grants for the 179 people who, almost five years after Hurricane Katrina, have yet to get rebuilding money from Road Home.

Road Home, a program administered by the Louisiana Recovery Authority with money from the Department of Housing and Urban Development, took the determined value of the home and subtracted from it any insurance and FEMA money homeowners received. The difference, capped at a maximum $150,000, was then granted to eligible applicants.

Sounds simple. It might even sound fair. Until you consider that value isn't the same as cost and that two houses identical in every way but location could get disparate grants—even if the money needed to repair them is exactly the same.

Generally speaking, homes in black neighborhoods aren't valued as highly as homes in white neighborhoods— and not because the bricks, drywall, flooring and roofing materials used in their construction necessarily cost less. They are often considered of lower value simply because of what they are: homes in a black neighborhood.

If you base a rebuilding grant on a home's value and not its cost, and thousands get less money than others to buy an identical amount of Sheetrock, then your goal of rebuilding storm-ravaged cities and parishes hasn't been met. And according to Kennedy, it's likely you've violated the law.

"The Court does not take lightly that some African-American homeowners received lower awards than they would have if their homes were in predominantly white neighborhoods," Kennedy wrote in a July memorandum opinion. "And although the Court appreciates that all of the parties are committed to the rebuilding of a city that has suffered greatly, it is regrettable that this effort to do so appears to have proceeded in a manner that disadvantaged African-American homeowners who wish to repair their homes." However, he said law prevents the federal government from telling a state how it should have handled money already spent. But he can order Louisiana to use a different calculation for the remaining 179 people in line.

Damon Hewitt, a lawyer with the NAACP Legal Defense Fund and Educational Fund and a New Orleans native, said Thursday that plaintiffs were seeking relief for everybody who got shorted by the Road Home's formula, not just the black applicants. Though the five plaintiffs are all black, a white or Vietnamese person living in one of their neighborhoods would be equally harmed by such a formula. The formula would likely give a white homeowner in St. Bernard Parish less money than the owner of an identical house in Lakeview. "It's difficult when you have a claim that says race, race, race" to get people to see that it's not an exclusively racial issue, he said, but that approach was necessary.

The plaintiffs' original complaint estimates that 20,000 black New Orleans homeowners got less than they should have, but Hewitt said that number becomes larger if all races in all parishes are included.

"We have a race claim, but there really wasn't another claim to bring," Hewitt said. "The law doesn't often give you a way to address complex problems." Addressing black homeowners' complaints, he said, would mean the state "would essentially have to fix this for everyone. We would love to see recalculation of grants for every homeowner in the state. We brought it on behalf of African-American homeowners," but we were hoping for an "LRA/HUD settlement that would lift all boats."

"There's no one lawsuit that could have addressed all the problems" with the Road Home Program, Hewitt said.

Apparently not. This lawsuit was theoretically successful. And essentially it does nothing.

CAN ORLEANS SCHOOLS THRIVE IN DEMOCRACY?

SEPTEMBER 14, 2010

Is democracy incompatible with good public schools? Or is it that democracy is incompatible with good public schools in New Orleans?

There will be no way around those questions as State Superintendent Paul Pastorek and the Board of Elementary and Secondary Education decide if the state should return some of the schools it's running back to the locally elected Orleans Parish School Board

Pastorek is reportedly willing to cede control of some Recovery School District campuses back to the school board in the near future, but he isn't willing to cede that control right now. He is expected to announce his recommendations at the BESE meeting in Baton Rouge today, and that board is scheduled to vote on the matter Dec. 9. There will be a public hearing on the issue in the McDonogh 35 High School auditorium on Oct. 14.

History tells us that those meetings will be intense. There will be yelling. There will be insults thrown around like bricks. There will be lots of heat, if precious little illumination.

That brings us back to where we began: Is democracy incompatible with good public schools? Is New Orleans the single jurisdiction in Louisiana where the two concepts are thought to be in opposition to one another?

Understand, anybody who tells you the pre-Katrina Orleans Parish School Board had made a good case for democracy is a liar. The truth ain't in 'em. Our schools were mostly awful. The system's finances were even worse, and the board members were hostile to the very idea that they had anything to do with the way things were. Ellenese Brooks-Simms, the president of the board who later pleaded guilty to bribery charges, liked to blame the poverty of its students for the school system's woeful performance.

Yes, the students depending on New Orleans schools were mostly poor, and only a fool would believe that poverty brings with it no consequences, but that demographic tidbit was always being waved around by Brooks-Simms as a means to deflect blame from herself and the other board members. And you know what happened to Brooks-Simms, an elected official who had once seemed so indomitable? Without voters even knowing that she was suspected in a bribery scheme, she got bounced in a 2004 re-election bid where 84 percent of those voting chose somebody else. Another blame-avoiding board member was opposed by 71 percent of the voters. Yet, another incumbent saw the writing on the wall and dropped out of the race before voters got the opportunity to put her out of office.

The schools hadn't exactly been transformed by the time of Hurricane Katrina; some might argue that board members elected in 2004 weren't that great either. Still, there is no disputing the point that in the last election before the hurricane, New Orleans voters saw that they were being ill-served by certain school board

members and sent them packing. There are New Orleans schools that remain academically unacceptable five
years after the state took them over, but local residents
cannot toss out the people they deem responsible for
those continuing failures.

Pastorek deserves much credit for the work he's done
making school systems around the state more accountable, but it's ironic to hear of his plan to require schools
to prove their academic mettle before they can leave
the Recovery School District. If they haven't yet proved
themselves academically, isn't that the fault of the RSD?
If those schools continue to fail while being managed
by the RSD, what then?

That's what Deirdre Johnson Burel, executive director
of Orleans Public Education Network, was alluding to
when she said residents are frustrated by "the lack of
meaningful direct ways for the community's voice to
be heard."

There are other voices, though, that express reserva-
tions about quickly going back to the way things were.
Andre Perry, who oversees four UNO charters, says
that the school board needs to first prove that it can
turn around failing schools before we go back to what
we had. But if Pastorek maintains his position that he'll
keep control over failing schools, the school board
will never get to prove that it can turn around failing
schools.

Turning all our schools into successful ones should
be our goal. The question remains: Can we manage
that important job with a local, democratically elected
board?

APATHY BLIGHTS SLAIN CHILDREN'S MEMORIALS

OCTOBER 31, 2010

Even the memorials to our slain children are blighted. At least the one erected to honor Dwight "Mikey" Stewart, a 1994 victim of a drive-by shooting, is. Walk up to the corner of Second and South Johnson streets, and it's doubtful that you'll see anything commemorating the four-year existence of a little boy whose reputation for liking food earned him the name "Mikey," like the tot in the classic Life cereal commercial.

The memorial only became visible to me after Al Mims, a state parole board member and crusader against violence perpetrated against children, picked up a stick from the trash-strewn ground and whacked at the weeds and tall grass.

And there it was: a waist-high monument that wouldn't have been out of place in a graveyard. The engraved dates reveal that the child hadn't reached his fifth birthday. As if to emphasize that point, a pair of Mikey's tennis shoes, cast in bronze, shows how tiny this victim of gun violence was when a local gunslinger put a gaping hole in his chest.

The day he was killed his mother, Deljuana Stewart, told The Times-Picayune that the location of his wound made it impossible for her baby to even cry out in pain. "He had a big hole in his chest," she said. "He couldn't say anything. He couldn't even cry. He just stared at me."

It's 16 years later, and I'm standing in "Mikey's Garden," a small lot that was announced as a blooming reminder of a life cut short but has become just one more overgrown, unsightly mess. A man pedaling along Second Street asks me if my presence means the grass is about to be cut. Does he want the garden fixed up so passersby can remember it as the site where an innocent little boy was killed?

No. He wants it cut because, he explains, he can't see cars approaching on Johnson if he's riding on Second.

Mims is disgusted at the state of the park and what he thinks it symbolizes: a city that raises its voice in anger and anguish when a child is slain, marks the spot in an act of remembrance and then forgets.

After 2-year-old Jeremy Galmon was killed in a drive-by at First and Dryades last month, somebody erected a cross decorated with children's palm prints. Jeremy Galmon's name is printed on the cross, along with a quote from Isaiah: "and a little child shall lead them."

What's Jeremy's memorial going to look like two, three, four years from now, Mims wonders. And what about Kevin Wooden or the baby who got his throat slashed because his daddy didn't want to pay child support? We still think of them? Ishmael Combre was killed after he tried to rescue his mother from a beating. Her boyfriend "broke the knife in the boy's head," Mims reminds me, and church folks—"they had just come from prayer!"—stood frozen and watched it.

Mims isn't anti-church. Church is where we met. He's just anti-doing nothing as kids are being cut down.

"I would like to see this cleaned up," he says. "I just want the public to see you can't forget."

In 2004 I wrote a column that mentioned a street sign on Carrollton Avenue being dedicated to Kevin Wooden, a 6-year-old who was beaten and left to die a slow death in an Uptown storage facility in February 1999. Yet, when Mims mentioned Wooden's memorial, nothing registered. And I drive past the sign twice a day: on my way to work and back home.

In January 2009 Ja'Shawn Powell's body was stuffed in an athletic bag—by his father, authorities say—and discarded in a yard adjacent to Van McMurray Park. A grand jury indicted the boy's father, Danny Platt, on a first-degree murder charge in April 2009. "I'm sorry about killing my baby," he said to reporters as he was being led to jail, though he denied the police version that avoiding child support was his motivation.

I saw no memorial for Ja'Shawn Friday morning. A security guard working nearby said he'd never seen one there. But he had seen the one for Jeremy, a few blocks away, he said.

At Mikey's memorial his shoes sit on a box filled with crushed guns and cemented shut. The symbolism is nice. So is the idea of a garden.

But if "Mikey's Garden" remains another abandoned lot with towering weeds, we'll be allowing one of our problems to help us avoid thinking about another.

EX-COP HAS A TIRED EXCUSE FOR ATROCITY

Gregory McRae is a former New Orleans police officer on trial in federal court for incinerating a New Orleans man's body in a Chevrolet Malibu the Friday after Hurricane Katrina.

NOVEMBER 12, 2010

McRae did it. We don't have to wait for the jury to decide that. The first thing McRae's attorney, Frank DeSalvo, did when he stood up before the jury Wednesday morning was admit that his client did just what federal prosecutors say he did. McRae drove the car to the Algiers levee. He lit a flare, threw it in the car with Henry Glover's body and walked away. McRae also fired a shot into the rear window of the car, his attorney said.

DeSalvo will ask the jury to acquit his client on the grounds that he was sleepy. McRae reported to work Sunday, Aug. 28—the day before Hurricane Katrina hit the Gulf Coast—and, according to DeSalvo, had not had a single minute's sleep when he burned up Glover's body Friday morning. His job that week was fixing all

the equipment—from trucks to boat motors to chain-
saws—that his colleagues needed on their rescue and
cleanup missions.

After McRae worked that superhuman single shift of
more than 100 hours, he apparently was not in his right
mind. "He made a very bad decision," DeSalvo told the
jury, but he insists his client was not trying to violate
anybody's civil rights. "He just set that car on fire."

Prosecutors say former officer David Warren was
wrong to shoot Glover outside an Algiers strip mall that
Friday morning. They accuse McRae and Lt. Dwayne
Scheuermann of beating and kicking two men seeking
medical attention for Glover at Paul B. Habans Elementary and then burning Glover's body on the levee.
They accuse retired Lt. Robert Italiano and Lt. Travis
McCabe of obstructing justice by writing a false report
regarding Glover's death and disappearance and then
lying to the FBI about it.

The car that was burned along with Glover belonged
to William Tanner. He didn't know Glover. He was a
Good Samaritan who stopped when he saw a wounded
man on the ground and took Glover and his brother
to the police. Tanner says he was beaten. He watched
the police drive off in his car with Glover's body on the
back seat.

Wednesday morning, lawyers for the four other defendants were united in denying that their clients
had done anything wrong. Though he trailed McRae
to the levee in a truck, Scheuermann's defense is that
he had no clue that McRae would set fire to Glover's
body. DeSalvo was the only one who said that his client had indeed done what the government alleged. He
didn't address the allegation that McRae beat the two

men who sought help for Glover but admitted that he drove Glover's body away from a police compound and torched it.

God help us all if a storm gives our police the right to desecrate our bodies.

Knowing that the defendants' lawyers were going to insist that the chaos after Katrina mitigates the defendants' actions, Assistant U.S. Attorney Tracey Knight told the jury first: "Some actions are never excusable."

DeSalvo, the second defense attorney to address the jury Wednesday, asked that jurors take into account the events of the preceding week and the impact they had on McRae's thoughts, emotions and decisions. He had seen "floating, bloated, decaying bodies" that week, DeSalvo told the jury. Reinforcements arrived at the police compound that Friday afternoon, DeSalvo said, and his client was finally able to end that shift of his that had gone uninterrupted since Sunday, but as everything was unfolding that morning, McRae was unaware that help was on the way. That was his mindset. He had to take care of things himself.

McRae was so focused on getting the job done himself that, according to his attorney, he took a brand new set of tools out of Tanner's Malibu before he destroyed the car. McRae knew the tools had been looted, DeSalvo said, because they were so shiny and new. As the "motorhead" around the place, McRae knew he could put those tools to good use fixing motors and such.

DeSalvo seemed oblivious to what that says about his client. There was a body in William Tanner's car and a brand new set of tools.

Greg McRae deemed only the tool set worth preserving.

NAACP SHOULDN'T GIVE DEFILLO A PASS

JULY 8, 2011

You used to be able to count on the NAACP to take up the cause of a slaughtered black man.

Especially, say, if that black man was shot in the back by police. If the police then burned up the victim's body, you could be sure that the National Association for the Advancement of Colored People would call for the punishment of every officer involved, including police brass with knowledge of the crime who chose to look the other way.

At the New Orleans Police Department, Assistant Superintendent Marlon Defillo looked the other way in June 2008 when an outside law enforcement officer told him New Orleans police may have killed a man and incinerated his body days after Hurricane Katrina. He got the name Henry Glover from the coroner's office, but for seven months, Defillo has testified under oath, he made no attempt to find out what happened. Meanwhile, Glover's family pined for justice.

If I told you that the NAACP's New Orleans branch has a link on its website urging the removal of a top New Orleans police officer, you might guess the group's targeting Defillo for initially refusing to investigate the reported murder of a black man. But you'd have guessed wrong. It's Police Superintendent Ronal Serpas the civil rights group wants ousted because some officers in Serpas' inner circle profited from an improperly formed police detail.

Serpas, who has made the termination of lying officers a centerpiece of his reform efforts, hasn't been convincing when he says he didn't know that his son-in-law, his bodyguard and one of his closest friends were all getting paid through a detail that the close friend improperly created. But even if one could prove that Serpas has been lying, his offense still wouldn't compare to what Defillo, the department's second-in-command, admits he did: look the other way and let the killing of a man go uninvestigated.

This selective outrage makes the NAACP look petty and more interested in political gamesmanship than the advancement of its people. It leaves the group wide open to the accusation that it wants Serpas out because he's white and that it's been silent on Defillo because he's black.

Danatus King, president of the New Orleans branch of the NAACP, said Thursday that the call for Serpas' removal arose from the group's membership. Every dues-paying member of the chapter has the right to bring up such an issue for a vote, he said, and if a majority supports it, that becomes the local NAACP's position. Serpas was brought up for a vote. "No, we haven't taken a position on Defillo," he said. Nobody in the membership has made him an issue.

Is King concerned at how that looks: a dead black body on one side, a few officers stuffing their pockets on the other, and the NAACP fixates on the ill-gotten cash? He said those concerned about what the local

NAACP is doing or not doing can join the group and advocate for the positions dear to them.

One might expect a little more leadership from the top. Surely King and the other leaders of the group could find a way to make Defillo's removal an issue if they thought he deserved to be removed.

Even so, there are more than 500 members in the local chapter, King said. If, in such a large group, there's not a single person who's disturbed enough by Defillo's inaction to call for his removal—if we've reached the point where not even the NAACP seems to care about victims such as Glover—what's left for us to do but despair?

FOR A SLAIN INNOCENT, JUSTICE AND TEARS

AUGUST 7, 2011

Dear Ronald,

We never met. Truth is, I never even knew of your existence when you were alive. But this being New Orleans, it turns out that I know people who know your people. They've got nothing but positive things to say about all of you Madisons.

You didn't choose the family you were born into, Ronald. None of us do. But you and your big brother Lance demonstrate how important it can be to have a family with a rock-solid reputation. The Sunday after Hurricane Katrina, you were chased down like wild game and blasted in the back by a shotgun-toting New Orleans police officer. Your brother was accused of trying to kill a whole truckload of police. It didn't make sense, Ronald. Nobody who knew the two of you and y'all's family could imagine you threatening the police.

Especially you. The calendar said you were 40 years old, but your mind said otherwise. You were really a child, with a child's unwavering attachment to your dachshunds, Bobbi and Sushi. It's why you were in New Orleans to begin with. None of the hotels your family called before evacuating would take your pets, and separating you from them was hardly an option. So Lance, who was tired anyway from long hours at FedEx, stayed with you. He took care of you as you cried during the scary storm.

Kenneth Bowen, Robert Faulcon, Robert Gisevius and Anthony Villavaso, the bad people who killed you and 17-year-old James Brissette, badly wounded four other people, caused your brother to go to jail and lied about what happened there on the Danziger Bridge, were all found guilty Friday, Ronald. They're going to go to prison, we all hope for a very long time.

U.S. Attorney Jim Letten said after the verdicts that vulnerable people like you, Ronald, deserved the "police's protection, not their abuse." Yet, Faulcon, the officer who took the witness stand and admitted to shooting you, said that as he approached you from behind, he didn't even tell you to stop running or yell out "Police!"

You were, as prosecutor Barbara "Bobbi" Bernstein put it, "unarmed, already wounded, disabled and running away." Faulcon kept his silence and pulled the trigger on you anyway.

It's impossible, Ronald, for any of us to hurt the way your family hurts, but you should know that all of New Orleans was made a victim by what those officers did to you and your brother, to James, Jose Holmes and Susan, Leonard and Lesha Bartholomew.

Mr. Letten said that "the citizens of this country should not have to fear the people sworn to protect them," but our collective fear of the New Orleans Police Department reached new heights once we learned how the police had killed you, Ronald, and how they tried to cover up their crimes so that y'all who got shot or shot at would look like you deserved it.

Sgt. Arthur Kaufman, who helped organize that cover-up, will also be going to prison. So will five other officers who did bad things but chose to admit what they did before things got worse for them.

Your family kept it together Friday, Ronald. At least outside the federal courthouse they did. Lance and your sister Jacquelyn Madison Brown read prepared statements thanking prosecutors and the jurors for doing right by you in finding the accused officers guilty.

James Brissette's mother, Sherrel Johnson, wasn't so dispassionate. She radiated anger and relief, sorrow and satisfaction. The police robbed her of her son, she said. James, she said, is "gonna forever more be an urn of ashes."

"They took the twinkle out my eye, the song out of my heart and blew out my candle. But it's gon' be alright—because justice has been served. The day has come. Fat lady done sang. Curtain came down. Nothing more to say."

But maybe there is something more to say, Ronald.

New Orleans failed you. It failed James and everybody else shot at on the bridge that day. Friday's verdict doesn't bring y'all back, and it doesn't heal any physical wounds. But perhaps it signals to police that a new era has arrived, one that demands that they follow the law the same as all of us.

AN EMPTY WALLET IS A TERRIFYING THING

I walked into a local Department of Motor Vehicles office shortly after 8 a.m. Tuesday. I was back in my car with a renewed license before the bottom of the hour.

That's one of those remarkable occurrences you feel you've got to tell the whole world about. And, believe me, I did. Well, that small fraction of the world that I encountered the rest of that day.

It occurred to me later, though, that the amount of time I spent at the DMV wasn't nearly as significant as how I paid for my new ID. On the drive between my house and the DMV, I stopped at an ATM and withdrew two twenties.

Four years ago, I wasn't able to renew my license until I had first taken a jar of coins to Sav-a-Center. My checking account wasn't overdrawn, but neither was there enough there for me to visit an ATM. I had to scavenge for change before resorting to a coin-counting machine that swallowed up 8 cents of every dollar.

I was Katrina poor. I had a mortgage. I had rent. I had a car note, something I didn't have when floodwaters swallowed up my truck. I had no more savings. That week in September 2007—two years after the storm, five months before Road Home paid me and I paid off the mortgage—was, financially speaking, my post-Katrina low point.

I kept quiet about my financial distress. I'm sure I could have gone to a friend and secured a $20 loan till that week's payday. After all, what's $20? But that was the irony. Needing an amount so small made me too embarrassed to ask for it.

"How I Got Over," the classic gospel recording proclaims. "How I got over. My soul looks back and wonders how I got over." For those of us who are still here and still standing more than six years after Katrina, what better describes our sense of awe at having arrived at this point?

There's a humility in those lyrics. Songwriters Clara Ward and Dorothy Pearson and the many gospel artists who've performed the song—this city's Mahalia Jackson included—aren't crediting themselves for how far they've come. They are, instead, acknowledging that they had nothing to do with the progress they've made and that if it were left up to them, they may not have got over at all.

According to a recent report, the poverty rate in America is the highest it's been since 1993. There are, according to the U.S. Census Bureau, 46.2 million people in America living beneath the poverty line, the highest number in the 52 years the agency has been publishing those figures. That high number of poor people is scary in and of itself, but it's even scarier when one looks at it more closely. What's the definition of poverty? It's a family of four earning $22,314 a year.

Another report reveals that in Louisiana, many of our children are occasionally going without food. The Food Research and Action Center, a national anti-hunger group, found that New Orleans ranked eighth highest among cities, and Louisiana ranked seventh highest among states for children suffering "food hardship."

Another group, Feeding America, reported that 18 percent of children in Louisiana are "food insecure." Their families either worried that their food would run out, bought food that ran out, or they ate less than they otherwise would have so that their food wouldn't run out.

Gov. Bobby Jindal told an audience at the Tchefuncta Country Club Monday that Louisiana is doing well economically because it "chose to make tough choices" during his tenure. One of those choices made was the slashing of the state's budget for food pantries by 90 percent: from $5 million to $500,000. Before the cuts were announced in 2009, Louisiana food pantries had been serving 7 million meals a year. It's no wonder, then, that so many Louisianans reported being hungry in 2010.

The stress of Hurricane Katrina never put me beneath the poverty line. But living through those lean days made me aware of how easy it can be to fall into trouble, how terrifying it can be when you have to reach for your jar of nickels and dimes to take care of a necessary expense.

ROOM FOR BLACK LEADERS IN CHARTER MOVEMENT?

DECEMBER 18, 2011

I've never said this to Marie Gould, who runs the reading buddy program at Benjamin Banneker Elementary School, but I show up week after week, year after year to read with students partly because I want to topple any misconceptions they may have developed that reading is a white thing. Or—given the fact that I've mostly read with boys—that it's a girl thing.

Most of the volunteers who participate in the program come to Banneker from nearby Tulane and, thus, reflect the racial make-up of the university. White or black, we're all there for the same reason: to help the children at Banneker improve their reading and, by extension, pass the state's high-stakes exam. I deserve no more praise for showing up than they do.

But I think my failure to show up would be worse. How many chances would my buddies get to see a black man reading—reading to them one-on-one at that? That's why I'm there. It's more than volunteerism. I hope it's a preventive against the racial self-questioning that so often confronts young black students.

Erika McConduit, an executive vice president at the Urban League of Greater New Orleans, recently complained to a committee of the Board of Elementary and Secondary Education that the overwhelmingly black student population in New Orleans public schools doesn't see enough leaders who look like them. "There are disproportionate numbers of whites who are heading our schools and teaching our children," McConduit told the BESE committee that evaluates charter school applications.

McConduit's lament will surely be taken by some as an expression of anti-white hatred, but one can be as kumbaya as they come and still worry about the psychological effect on black children who come to equate both education and authority with whiteness.

The first two charters in the city—New Orleans Charter Middle School and Samuel J. Green Charter School—were started before Hurricane Katrina by a black psychologist, Tony Recasner. Yet, one gets the sense now that a sizeable number of black people see the charter school movement as a takeover attempt by white people—or, at the very least, a movement that's indifferent to the frustrations McConduit expressed. I asked Recasner Friday how we arrived at this point.

He hasn't seen any research that includes a racial breakdown of the teachers in the local charter schools, he said, and suggested such an inquiry could validate McConduit's concern. But even without the benefit of numbers, Recasner said a few things are contributing to the worry that school leadership is undergoing a racial transformation.

First, he said, there was the mass firing of public school teachers in New Orleans by the Orleans Parish School Board after Hurricane Katrina. Most of those fired were black. In college, dwindling numbers of black students are choosing education, he said, opting for more lucrative professions.

Many of the charter schools have exhibited a "selection bias," he said, preferring very young teachers who buy into a philosophy that puts them at school 12 hours a day. That, in and of itself, alienates veteran teachers with families, he said, but add to it the natural suspicion many veteran teachers have had for the very idea of charter schools. Many have chosen not to teach there. There's "a lot going on," he said, "but it's really not ill will" on the part of any of the charter school operators.

Recasner, who said he sought a teacher corps that was similar to those at other public schools, is no longer directly involved with charter schools. After serving as principal at the schools mentioned above, then as president of FirstLine Schools, Inc., which operates five schools in the city, he's now the CEO of Agenda For Children. Though he's no longer hands-on, Recasner said he imagines that every operator out there "would love to have a school where the majority would be young African-American teachers." He said, "Kids (would) get to see themselves" in their teachers and principals, and "it would make the work a lot less challenging."

Recasner seemed just as careful not to criticize white teachers as I am not to criticize the white students who volunteer as reading buddies, for it's not their presence around black children that's the problem. It's the relative absence of black people. "If we believe this is a bad thing," Recasner said, "how do we reverse the trend?" How do we "create a pipeline," he said, that will bring young black teachers to New Orleans?

SIGHT OF TINY CASKET IS HARD TO TAKE

DECEMBER 30, 2011

My column the Friday before Hurricane Katrina was an interview with Malcolm Gibson, a local mortician who, among other things, spoke of the difficulty of keeping the embalming fluid from leaking out of bodies perforated by bullets.

When Gibson and I talked we had no idea of the unprecedented sorrow the next week would bring. We talked about the killer we knew: New Orleans gun violence. The city had recorded 205 homicides in the eight months before the storm.

As of Thursday, this year's tally of homicides stood at 197, but the city has fewer people than it did six years ago. Things were bad before the storm, but Gibson senses that they're worse now. Before, he said, "You didn't kill babies. You didn't kill women." But such honor among murderers has disappeared.

Out of all of the year's carnage, we're most likely to remember the gunshot that killed Keira Holmes at the B.W. Cooper housing development on Dec. 18, four days before she would have turned 2. Police say Keira, also known as "Pooh Bear," was playing outdoors when she was shot in the head as four men were gunning for a 19-year-old. Gibson prepared her body for burial.

The toddler's slaying is the type that arouses the city's anger, he said, just like the 2009 killing of 6-year-old Four Overstreet and the 2010 quadruple murder of 25-year-old Angel Davis, her 7-year-old daughter, Jamaria Ross, her 4-year-old son, Joseph Davis, and Angel Davis' 17-year-old sister, Malekia Davis. Gibson prepared those five bodies, too, which may be why he was so confident Thursday that our anger over Keira will eventually subside—if it hasn't subsided already.

Those five deaths were all "high profile, but it's just not high profile enough," he said, to provoke sustained and effective outrage. Keira was killed a week before the holiday, and, as Gibson puts it, "Who wants to be mad at Christmas?"

It's the frustration one hears from just about everybody who witnesses the city's murder epidemic up close: Why is our grief so temporary? How do we forget dead babies so quickly?

You'd think, given the city's professed outrage, Gibson said, that more people would have contributed money as Keira's family struggled to meet her burial expenses. But her death produced more talk than help. There were some memorable exceptions. There was the tearful man who walked in off Elysian Fields, handed over $25 and said, "Here, this is for the little girl." There was the teller at the bank who had to wait till payday to make a $20 donation and held Gibson up for 30 minutes talking about her own 1-year-old at home. While more donations may have reflected a stronger commitment from the public, ultimately, Gibson said, "If we didn't get a dollar, we were going to bury the little girl."

Undertakers have to know the science of preserving bodies. They also have to know the art of comforting families. How to do that when the victim is a child?

It's not easy, Gibson said, if for no other reason than parents never expect to plan funerals for their children. "Weddings, graduation parties, that's what we plan," he said, "but funerals?"

"They're looking like, 'I can't believe I'm doing this,'" when they're trying to plan the service, Gibson said. Time has taught him what not to say. For example: "What casket would you like?" That's likely to get this response: "I'd like none of them. I'd like not to be talking to you." He found out from Keira's mother that the little girl liked pink. At that point, he said, "(I'm) not gonna talk casket. I'm gonna talk pink."

I imagined that the sight of a tiny casket would be hard for anybody to take. I went to Gibson's office partly because I wanted the jolt of seeing the dimensions for myself. However, Gibson shows grieving families a catalog prepared by Cherokee Casket Company, which specializes in caskets for babies and children.

The catalog serves the family's interests and his own because apparently there are things even an undertaker in New Orleans couldn't bear.

"I can't imagine bringing someone into a room of children's caskets," Gibson said. "You hope that's not how you make your money."

JEFFERSON CAN EXPECT A SLEEPLESS NIGHT

MAY 4, 2012

He was born poor in one of the nation's most forsaken places, received a legal education at one of the world's most exclusive universities and became a stand-out during his nine terms in the U.S. House of Representatives. But all of that—the poverty of Lake Providence, the prestige of Harvard Law School, the power of the Ways and Means Committee—is now in William Jefferson's past. Today the 65-year-old becomes a federal prisoner. He's been sentenced to 13 years.

The evidence of his corruption was overwhelming. During his trial in 2009 even his attorney acknowledged that receiving a briefcase with $100,000 and promising to bribe a Nigerian vice president was "stupid," an "exercise in poor judgment," unethical and not appropriate.

For all those reasons—and for his continued insistence that he broke no law—there will be some cheers when Jefferson reports to prison today.

But there ought to be sadness, too. For Louisiana, from which some public official seems to always be headed to jail. And for the people, those who were inspired by Jefferson's ascent and devastated by his fall.

He let people down.

Oliver Thomas knows what that feels like. The former New Orleans city councilman was so popular he was all but guaranteed to succeed Ray Nagin as mayor till that bombshell announcement in August 2007 that he had taken a bribe and was cooperating with the federal government.

Thomas, sentenced to 37 months, reported to prison Jan. 3, 2008. It was a humiliating experience, he said over breakfast Thursday: having to get naked, bend over and "open up your butt." For the first six days he was allotted an hour a day outside his cell and allowed one shower that entire time.

But it wasn't when he talked about his confinement that Thomas' eyes watered. He thinks prison made him better. His emotions bubbled up when he talked about the hurt he caused, not just to himself and his family but to those nameless supporters who'd expected more of him.

One of his good friends, he said, a man not given to profanity, "really let me have it." Even as he hurled expletives, the friend argued that Thomas had always shown concern for those on the bottom rungs.

"What we got now?!" he yelled. "What are we going to do now? You (messed) up, and it's (messed) us up!"

"I hung up the phone and cried," Thomas said.

Mary Landrieu lectured him. His crimes were being exposed two years after Hurricane Katrina, when New Orleans still needed help from all over: from the state, from the feds, from philanthropists, from volunteers. "We didn't need another black eye," the senator told him.

But that's not all she said. She added, "I'm here for your family if they need me."

"I didn't think I deserved that," Thomas said. "I was not emotionally prepared for support. You don't feel that good about yourself. I didn't want to be a good person. I'd rather you say I was a bad person."

Like Jefferson, Thomas' origins were humble. Oliver Thomas Sr. worked as a laborer and janitor for the city. He acquired no money and told Oliver Jr. that the only thing he could give him was a good name, his own name.

More water in the eyes.

"Damn, the only thing you could give me, I destroyed," Thomas said.

"You can get used to the public scorn," he said, "but when you feel like you've let down the people close to you, that takes time."

Our conversation was forever being interrupted Thursday by people shaking Thomas' hand and asking his opinion or for some kind of help. There are people who've never stopped rooting for him. Just as there are some who viewed his punishment with pleasure.

"It's the Roman Coliseum. They want you to be de-voured," he said, unaware that "the fact that you've let yourself down" hurts more than any jeers.

"But in some ways, when you violate the public trust, you deserve it," he said, "because the public's your life."

His advice to Jefferson?

"Leave your title at the door. Start the rebirthing pro-cess. There's work to be done in prison." If you talk to them and don't try to show yourself to be superior, he said, other inmates "can even benefit from your down-fall."

What is it like the day after check-in? What does he feel when he wakes up?

"Wake up?!" He snorted. "I didn't go to sleep."

CHANCE ENCOUNTER, CHANGED LIFE

MAY 18, 2012

Troy Simon was pedaling Magazine Street, tap shoes on his back, heading to the French Quarter where he knew he could make as much as $100 a day. He knew, too, of more illicit hustles—he'd sold weed, he'd stolen copper—but his grandmother had been talking to him about Jesus, and Troy, then 14, had prayed for help escaping his life of delinquency. The streets were thronged. It was Carnival 2008. There was money to be made on Bourbon Street.

If Troy hadn't pedaled by a former teacher that day, would he be graduating from Sci Academy June 1? Would the kid who once lived in an abandoned apartment, the teenager who couldn't read worth anything, be making plans for a dorm at New York's Bard College or a career as an English teacher?

As focused and self-possessed as the 18-year-old is today, it's hard to imagine Troy needing to have crossed paths with anybody to get on the road to success. Still, his biking past Sarah Bliss after an Uptown parade is textbook serendipity. She called out to him and immediately pulled him into a network of Teach For America teachers who resumed the work they'd begun with Troy when he was in Houston after the storm.

He remembers that fifth-grade year at New Orleans West College Prep (a KIPP school that evacuated to Houston) as the first time teachers told him, "We're going to help you accomplish your goals."

And not just pass him along?

"Second grade, I don't know how I made it to third grade," he said. "Third grade, I don't know how I made it to fourth grade."

It wasn't because he could read. He didn't recognize any words, not even cat or dog. Predictably, he failed LEAP. But he was too old to be held back again.

Nicole Cummins, his fifth-grade reading teacher, wondered, "How could this have happened? How could a kid get this far behind?" Despite his skills being "incredibly deficient"—a team including Bliss and Ben Ochstein started Troy on phonics—Cummins saw something special in him that "made me want to make sure that he didn't slip through any more cracks."

And yet, he did. He was arrested several times when he came back to New Orleans. In seventh grade he wore an ankle bracelet. As a peddler of marijuana, he had to decide if he was going to take the next step: push crack.

He knew, "Once I make that decision there's actually no backing out." So that's where he stopped. Others were expecting him to live a gangsta life, but Troy was honest with himself: "I didn't have the skills."

But nor did he have the skills to do the right thing, which is why his encounter with Bliss was like a prayer answered.

"He really just wanted to learn to read," she said. "He wanted to pass LEAP." She offered him tutoring, and he said, "Ms. Bliss, I want to take you up on your offer."

Troy can read now, well enough to have made it through New Orleans Charter Science and Math Academy, well enough to have earned admission to college. But not as well as he'd like.

"He knows that he's behind," Bliss said, but he has acquired "scholar habits." She remains amazed that Troy's "favorite thing to do is to go to the library and read the dictionary on weekends."

He won a scholarship from the Posse Foundation, which identifies students whose potential exceeds their test scores. That's how he's going to Bard. It will be hard, Cummins said, "but Troy now has the self-narrative, 'I can do hard things,' which is half the battle."

Troy was one of the 37 young people former President Bill Clinton addressed last week as they graduated from Urban League College Track. That program and Upward Bound at Xavier helped him play catch up.

"With my background, where I come from, I never thought I'd meet a president," Troy said Sunday. Clinton told them he'd been the first in his family to go to college, a point not lost on Troy.

During that May 10 ceremony, Troy pulled on his tap shoes and performed—for perhaps the last time. He was sending the audience a message.

"I'm not a tap dancer anymore. I'm not illiterate anymore."

OSCAR NIGHT TWEETS PUT CRUELTY ON DISPLAY

FEBRUARY 27, 2013

Dear Naomi,

Last week, when your mother and I left you in the care of a sweet older couple we know, the grandfatherly gentleman looked at your mother and me and decided you were too cute to have come from either of us. We both laughed, and I said, "You're right."

You are cute, Naomi, and though I know a 5-month-old doesn't yet understand words, when I tell you "You're so cute" over and over again, you expose all your gums, reveal your dimples and cover your eyes with your knuckles as if to say, "Oh, Daddy, stop it!"

But I won't stop. There are many things I'm required to do for you: clothe you, feed you, change you, provide you shelter. But it seems no less important for me as your dad to tell you you're beautiful. It's not hard to do. In fact, I tell you first and foremost because the truth compels me. But there's another reason beyond the obvious reality.

You have entered a world that won't be as kind to you as the couple that sat with you last week, and though Daddy intends to shield you from as many mean people as he can, some of them will get to you. They won't just neglect to say you're pretty. They'll insist that you are ugly. They'll tell you that something on you—your lips, your hips, your thighs, your bottom—is too big and that you ought to be ashamed of yourself. It's my job to reach you before they reach you, to help you build up a sense of worth that can't be easily toppled.

I've met black women, Naomi, beautiful women, who haven't managed to deflect those insults but have absorbed them and accepted them as true. You'll be different, won't you, sweetie? Tell me that when your body, your face, your hair are nitpicked and derided that you will channel Mississippi poet Sinclair O. Lewis, who wrote "Anyone Who Rejects Me Gotta Be Crazy."

There are crazy people out there, Naomi. I write this letter the day after Michelle Obama, wife of the president of the United States, made an appearance on the Oscars. In a night that features movie stars, Mrs. Obama, in a silver dress by designer Naeem Khan, was as glamorous as any of the women who walked the red carpet. Few women are as well-toned and shapely as she is.

Even so, you could go to Twitter and see her referred to as Moochelle. She was called fatty and likened to a gorilla. Some of the language was so offensive, so shockingly and blatantly sexist and racist, that I won't repeat it for you. You'll be introduced to those words soon enough, but right now you're a little girl.

Quvenzhané Wallis is a little girl, too, and like you, Naomi, she's black. She played Hushpuppy in "Beasts of the Southern Wild," and at 9, she was the youngest person ever to be nominated for a Best Actress award. She didn't win, but there are worse things in the world than not winning an award.

Sunday night, somebody tweeting for The Onion, a satirical news site I respect, described Quvenzhané as a four-letter word that begins with a c. It's one of the ugliest words in the language, sweetie, and it's unthinkable that an adult would think of it to describe anybody, let alone a child.

The tweet prompted what seems to be an unprecedented apology from the site. CEO Steve Hannah said those responsible would be disciplined. "Miss Wallis," he wrote, "you are young and talented and deserve better. All of us at The Onion are deeply sorry."

Whenever she saw the camera on her Sunday night, Quvenzhané raised her arms and flexed her biceps. That's what Hushpuppy did in the movie as her dad pushed her to be strong. He knew he wouldn't always be around to protect her and that she'd have to learn to be tough. Flexing your biceps isn't the only way to be strong, Naomi. If you can maintain your sense of worth and beauty in a world that insists you have none, you'll have exhibited more strength than a muscular pose ever could.

MARGARET WASHINGTON TALKS ABOUT LOSING HER PRINCESS, MARGUERITE LAJOY WASHINGTON

MAY 10, 2013*

Margaret Washington lost her daughter, Marguerite La-Joy Washington, Oct. 1, 2012. Marguerite was at her boyfriend's house in eastern New Orleans when, according to police, a former friend of her boyfriend fired shots into the bedroom window.

I got her when she was 3 months old. My son was about to complete his fourth year at Dillard, and I told him—I was a divorced mother—I said, "You're gonna get a little sister. You've always been the prince. I've always been the queen, and now we're gonna have a princess, and I want you to treat her that way."

As an adoptive parent, you take extra concern regarding the well-being of your child. Mothers will take a little liberty when the child goes out there to play, may-

---

* For Mother's Day 2013 I interviewed five New Orleans mothers who lost a child in a murder. This column, and the next four, are the result.

be not look back to see because they figure they're safe, but an adoptive parent is going to keep watching because you don't want anything to happen to this baby.

It was to be my granddaughter's 6th birthday, but at 7:10 in the morning the police came to my door. The female officer said, "Are you Margaret Washington?" I said, "Yes. What has happened?" I'm thinking a car accident or something because, see, my daughter was supposed to be at Dillard, in the dormitory.

My world turned inside out. I try not to be too emotional, but I just started whooping and hollering like somebody had hit me on the head—because it was disbelief. And then I get the story: that she's 12 blocks or more from my house with somebody that I don't know who is not a student. That just even overwhelmed me more.

When you hear about people being killed, young people, the first thing that comes to mind is that it's a male. But here you have gone to visit your boyfriend. You're just in the room visiting. There's a knock on the window. The boy responds, and bullets start flying.

The system is not a fair system. I have been to court six times. Motion for hearing. Motion for discovery. Sometimes the detective is not there. Sometimes the D.A. is not there. Then the next time, he doesn't have a public defender. So everything has been rescheduled and rescheduled. We are true victims in the whole process.

I don't look forward to Mother's Day. I didn't look forward to it for about 16 years because Mother had died, but I went through the motions of going to church every Mother's Day. This Sunday will be a little bit different, but I'm coming because my church has been there to sustain me through the loss.

Memories? Unless I become Alzheimer-y, they will never go away. So we just have to cling to those things and try to do what we can for others. The other thing is that Chanda (Burks) and I have gone to schools to try to talk to some of the children. You know we try to tell them, "Stop the violence."

If you got a friend that's not really your friend or something tells you maybe I shouldn't be with Johnny or James, listen. Run away, because if we don't tell them, who's gonna tell them?

CHANDA BURKS LOST HER SON JARED MICHAEL FRANCIS IN A TYPICALLY SHELTERED COMMUNITY

MAY 10, 2013

About 2:30 a.m. Sept. 15, Chanda Burks heard what sounded like fireworks outside her bedroom window in suburban Algiers. From her window she said she saw "a tall, skinny young man run off." She ran outside.

It was like a dead silence. I looked to my left and saw a figure lying on my lawn. I started from the bottom to the top, and I realized it was my son. I live in the Tall Timbers subdivision where nothing ever happens. This was our first murder. When I got to him he wasn't suffering or anything. He was just gasping.

Jared died at my house with me. One of my neighbors tried to resuscitate. At that point, I knew he was gone.

I know God was there. One, he brought him to die at home. Two, he didn't suffer. Three, I wasn't traumatized by it. It didn't leave me devastated to find my child in all this, and I was blessed that he was with me.

Jared Michael Francis, a senior at Edna Karr High School, was reportedly shot five times: in the chest, hand, leg and buttocks.

They had a conversation. The conversation went wrong. Jared raised his hand because the gun was coming out, and then he went to run. They shot him in the chest first, then he went to run across the street to my house, and he got shot in the leg and the behind. And then when he wouldn't die is when the guy reportedly stood over him and said, "You, b----, you better die," and then he left.

It's not a certain type. It could happen to anyone. Everybody should wake up to the fact that it can happen to them. It's a wake-up call to everybody. Because I live in one of the prime subdivisions where nothing ever happens, and something did happen. I'm not low income or poverty, and my son is gone. My son had dreams. He was a young entrepreneur on his own. So it's not a certain type of kid, and I think that's a wake-up call that a lot of people should have. And I think that through our (support) group, it's an awesome group, one thing I look forward to going on Thursdays. When we don't get to go on Thursdays we kind of have an attitude.

I have a great support system. I really do. But they don't understand where I'm coming from. (Looking at Shelia Johnson, whose son was also murdered) I know you said you feel like you're alone. When I get with my group, I don't have that feeling because I know they know where I'm coming from.

You know a lot of people spend their time telling me, "Time's gonna heal." I'm so tired of hearing people tell me that. I really am. Because at the end of the day, nobody knows what I think.

It takes my breath away to say my son was murdered.

A RECENT MURDER REMINDS SHARON CHARLES OF HER MURDERED SON, KENNETH MONROE

MAY 10, 2013

Most New Orleanians are likely to remember Dec. 11, 2008, because it snowed. It sticks out for Sharon Charles as the day her 27-year-old son, Kenneth Monroe, was likely murdered. Charles' phone didn't ring till Saturday. Kenneth's body and the bodies of two other men had been found in a 7th Ward house.

I was home that morning. Never slept that long in the morning in my life. It was like 11 or so. But the way I think about it? God allowed me to get as much rest as I could because he knew that I was gonna have a lot of sleepless nights.

And that was the morning I got a call, and somebody was saying, "You not going to the house?"

"To the house? What house? Who is this?"

"To the house where Kenny is. He's already expired." And I'm like, "Expired?" I know what that means.

He had been shot. My husband went to identify his body. A lot of things I didn't want to know at the time. I didn't want to know where and whatever, but he was shot. Three times. One in the head.

I try to think happy thoughts. It don't always come out happy thoughts because, I mean, it's still someone that you loved. That was my son. That was my only son. Again, it will be five years, but some days it seems like it was just yesterday. I think what has been my help is to be working in the work that I do, being at (Christian Unity Baptist) Church.

The young man that was killed Saturday? Down from the church? It was hard for me because the first person I thought about was his mother. (A passerby) on a bike was saying, "I know his mama. I know his mama and his daddy." My thought was now you have to go and tell his mother.

Then I found out through the news that he was the same age as my son, so that just floored me because I know where I was five years ago.

Losing a child, to me, I think that's the hardest pain that anybody could go through. I mean, I've lost my father... I've heard stories about, I'm not trying to downplay anybody's pain, but it's something about when you lose a child. It's just, it's, it's, it's just not like nothing that I think anybody could ever experience.

But then I think about our Lord and Savior. I think about what it was like for Mary when Jesus was being crucified, and I'm like, if Mary was able to, I guess I will be OK. These are the stories I tell myself to keep me moving. It don't always help because I still, I still fall out, I still feel. I don't sit up and look for a bad day, you know, but sometimes...

I'm just grateful that I can now talk about it because I can remember the times when I couldn't even say his name.

SHELIA JOHNSON'S SON, LARRY COLLIER JR., STRUGGLED MENTALLY BEFORE HE WAS MURDERED

MAY 10, 2013

Larry Collier Jr. was a Marine veteran who was diagnosed with paranoid schizophrenia a few years after his discharge. His mother, Shelia Johnson, struggled to get him help.

It's not something we dealt with as a family unit in the beginning because we thought, oh, you know, they don't know what they're talking about. We just were in denial, but as the years grew on and my son became older, I recognized the signs and the symptoms... He was less family oriented. He became a wanderer. In and out of jobs. In and out of the hospital. Me going to pick him up in several distant places. Destrehan, they had picked him up for loitering and trespassing. You know, he has like a long criminal past at Tulane and Broad, but it was all like misdemeanor charges because he was not getting the care that he needed. And he was on medicines: a shot twice a week and a pill once a day—when I could keep up with him.

But I couldn't keep up with him... He never regained a solid foundation in society. He just became a wanderer.

Sometimes he would allow me to talk to him. Sometimes he would come to my house, and he would stand across the street; he wouldn't approach me. He had that many mental issues.

So on July 1 (2011), he was killed.

On July 8 somebody called Johnson's ex-husband in Houston and said:

"Man, they got somebody in the paper with your name that's been killed." He said, "I know you not that young, so it can't be you. Do you have a son?"

His dad in turn called his mom here in New Orleans, and his mom called me. We met up, and we went to Rampart Street to the coroner's office, and we identified my son—after he had been dead seven days.

I heard pastor (talk) in church yesterday about a young man that was killed down from our church that lay on the ground literally for hours.

(In Larry's case) it is reported that somebody made a call to the police department at 2 something that morning. It was the Essence Festival. So I'm sure they were all gathered in a place that was more important than the Broadmoor area at that time. And they report that his body was found at 7:40 a.m. So I really felt it when pastor said that this child lay on the street for hours before anyone would even come to pick him up.

There's a victims against crime meeting. I went to one of those meetings, and it was kind of hard for me... I did get to talk with the detective supposedly working on the case, and they said they found his pockets turned inside out... It was the 1st, and he was getting a check from the government. He really didn't like using the bank. He had other issues, too. He drank. From his history at the hospital, he did indulge in some drugs.

So I did go to one of those, but I did feel like I was alone. I kinda felt like I sat at the table by myself. I met with the detective, but I didn't feel like it was something that I could really become involved in... I think that the people there maybe reached out and tried to, but I think my bitterness and my anger kind of put up a wall—so that I didn't want to be helped. I just wanted somebody to find out who took my son away. That was my sole goal.

I still ride by the site where they found his body. I bring flowers, but they're gone when you go back because it's right in front of someone's property.

He was a sweet kid. Very smart. He loved his daughter. He nurtured her when her mother wasn't there to do it. He'd be very proud of her graduating from high school next week. And I miss him. Every day. I pray that mothers, fathers, sisters, brothers, aunts, uncles, grandmothers never have to experience this.

Maybe my journey toward healing might come in trying to help other people who've experienced the same pain or some of the same. Some of what I've experienced and I live with daily, I don't know. Like I said, I have a lot of anger, and I don't know what'll take that away.

IONE BOLDEN STILL MISSES HER 2-YEAR-OLD SON, COREY, 34 YEARS LATER

MAY 10, 2013

When she was a 12-year-old girl, Ione Bolden's mother died of lupus. Six years later, Ione gave birth to a little boy. In October 1978, she was carrying the 2-year-old in her arms to a birthday party when, at the corner of Birch and Eagle streets, she heard shots. She clutched Corey to her and ran, but she soon felt something warm spilling through her fingers.

When I had Corey, it filled the void. It filled that void of my mother's absence. Because our house was quiet. My father was quiet. My grandmother was quiet. Everybody gone. Corey brought joy. He brought my Easter to me again and Christmas to me again. I was just as happy as he was for Christmas. I gave him what I enjoyed as a child. I never knew after two years he'd be gone.

It never goes away. It never does. That volunteer from out of town who was here, killed at Birch and Eagle? AmeriCorps? He was the second person after Corey killed on the very same corner. I was in my kitchen, looking up at the television, and it came on: Birch and

Eagle. You know, I do my research. He's the second. So I'm looking at Corey, who didn't get a chance to do the AmeriCorps. Who didn't ride the bike, who didn't go to the prom, who could have been a professional contributor to society.

(Joseph Massenburg's)* mother is (on) my path. Even though they live away. He was doing something positive. Here are two angels. One didn't get a chance to do that. One served in volunteerism. So it really brought back strong memories: Birch and Eagle Street.

I had a witness. Back in those times witnesses weren't as afraid to come forward as they are today. I think it's because (of) the growing number of weapons on the street. They have no regard for other people's lives. But also a failure in protection, failure in victims' protection programs.

People are living in fear today as opposed to during the era of Corey. And they have all rights to be, I suppose, because you can't even trust the people who are sent to serve and protect you. I mean, I hate to go there, but...

The graveyard is an interesting place. I find peace. I find comfort. So I will be there for Mother's Day because my mother and my child are there. I'm affected on both ends. He's resting between my mother and my father.

We never grow out of our grief. Look at me. '78. I still cry. I can pass a tree along Carrollton and just break down in tears. But I find my biggest comfort in the gravesite, and I'm gonna tell you why. I feel the wind picking up my hair. It's like they're coming out of the grave comforting me.

---

* Joseph Massenburg, an 18-year-old AmeriCorps volunteer, was killed on April 1, 2013, in what the police call a case of mistaken identity.

MURDER EPIDEMIC LEAVES US AT A LOSS FOR WORDS

MAY 22, 2013

Write about crime and murder in New Orleans with any regularity and you'll find yourself reaching for nouns. It happens to me just about every time.

I'm trying to convey the heartlessness, the nihilism, the depravity of young men aimlessly sending bullets into birthday parties and second-line parades, into the bodies of enemies and unsuspecting passersby, and I feel myself grasping for the right noun, something with a stronger emotional impact and a more provocative connotation than "man" or "teenager" or even "shooter" or "murderer."

I've used "gunmen," but that only applies to the single moment the subjects hold a piece of steel in their hands and doesn't seem to get at the essence of who they are. I've used "criminals," but the word doesn't seem adequate. Weed smokers are criminals. People who cheat on their taxes or shoplift lipstick or obstruct the sidewalks are criminals.

There have been times I've used "street toughs," but I fear that suggests a certain romanticism and that readers will picture the Fonz from "Happy Days" or the Sharks and the Jets from "West Side Story."

The word "thug" tempts me. Its origin as a word for predators in India who ambushed and strangled travelers would seem to make it perfect for the predators lurking on our streets. "Thug" has the added benefit of being the word most of the people spilling blood on our streets would most likely use for themselves. I've stayed away from it all the same. It's increasingly becoming weighted with race and used as code language.

After sitting by the hospital bed of his friend Deborah Cotton, New Orleans writer Brentin Mock, also a friend of mine, wrote a white-hot blog post asking, "What kind of animal shoots up a Mother's Day parade crowd? What kind of monster? I hate myself for thinking to ask this in these exact terms, but it's these exact terms in which I'm thinking."

But then the Los Angeles Times quoted him, and Brentin made attempts to tone it down. In a second blog post, he says, "At the time, I was trying to reconcile the anger I had inside of me, after spending hours in the hospital seeing my friend who was shot, with the more logical and humane response that should come after such a tragedy." If he hadn't had privileges that have been denied to so many young men on our streets, he writes, he himself may have become a monster.

I empathize with his struggle to choose the right noun and feeling dissatisfied with a choice. We are of a similar mind in that both of us want the public to become angry about the recurring violence, but we don't want the public to label the perpetrators as something less than human.

This isn't mere semantics. The nouns we choose reveal our relationship to the violent people we're talking about. The nouns we choose indicate whether we think they are redeemable or hopeless, reachable or incorrigible. The nouns we choose reveal what we think ought to happen to them when they transgress. It's not for nothing that prosecutors portray capital murder defendants as animals and monsters. You can't simultaneously acknowledge another's humanity and cast a vote to kill him.

My recent conversation with psychiatrist Dr. Denese Shervington about mothers mourning their murdered children turned out to provide as much insight about the murderers themselves. In her work with death-row inmates, Shervington said, she found a population with "no early experience of empathy or compassion." So there's no internal stop sign, no mental or emotional speed bump that prevents their anger from accelerating into a murderous rage.

While Shervington didn't profess a struggle with nouns, she did admit to having to work on herself before she could work on death row, asking, "How as a psychiatrist am I going to love you enough to work with you?"

Does my floundering about for the right noun derive from a similar struggle to see the perpetrators' humanity? I don't know.

I don't think about love as I write about them. I just want a noun that pegs them right but doesn't suggest they're less than human. Because if the psychiatrist is right, part of the reason these killers have become killers is that human beings who should have didn't treat them as such.

OUR DIFFERENCES CAN CREATE A RICH HARMONY

SEPTEMBER 1, 2013

Gov. Bobby Jindal thought the 50th anniversary of Martin Luther King Jr.'s speech at the March on Washington the perfect time to argue that Americans should stop thinking of race. "It's time to get over it," he writes for Politico.com. "Now that would be progress."

Would it really?

If King had dreamed of a country where our differences weren't noticed, he had the rhetorical gifts to express that. Instead, as he crescendoes through his finale, he imagines the day when "all of God's children, black men and white men, Jews and Gentiles, Protestants and Catholics, will be able to join hands and sing in the words of the old Negro spiritual, 'Free at last, Free at last, Thank God Almighty, We are free at last!'"

King doesn't dream of a world where men cease calling themselves black or white or stop identifying with their religion but a world where people live in harmony with others who are different. Musicians know that without difference there can be no harmony. Yet, as King laments, when it comes to human society, some people hear the "jangling discords of our nation" and suggest that the only solution is an imposition of sameness.

On its surface, it sounds kind of cool, everybody identifying as the same, nobody having a reason to reject anybody else. But it is, perhaps, the most pessimistic view of society there is, suggesting, as it does, that we can't be trusted to embrace folks who are different and are too small-minded and self-centered to co-exist with people unlike ourselves.

A colleague from my first job, a rural Southern white woman, said recently she doesn't see me as black. She's a sweet woman. I knew she meant that as praise. I tried to reflect her sweetness in my response. Being black is not shameful, and it's not something I expect my friends of other races to "get over" or look past. It's who I am. No, not all of who I am. It's not limiting. But it's a part of me. And I'll not deny that part of myself in exchange for anybody's friendship.

Jindal writes, "There is nothing wrong with people being proud of their different heritages. We have a long tradition of folks from all different backgrounds incorporating their traditions into the American experience, but we must resist the politically correct trend of changing the melting pot into a salad bowl. E pluribus Unum."

The governor says there's nothing wrong with having pride in one's heritage. However, he wags a finger at Americans who make a nod to their heritage in describing themselves. Asian-American, Cuban-American, African-American, Mexican-American, Indian-American? Jindal considers such compound descriptors an unacceptable emphasis on our "separateness."

How about just 'Americans?'" he asks. "That has a nice ring to it, if you ask me."

The maxim from "Animal Farm" comes to mind: "All animals are equal, but some animals are more equal than others." Not only does that sentence capture the growing inequality that developed in George Orwell's book, but it explains why some so-called hyphenated folk have had a harder time than others assimilating into America. They aren't as equal as the others.

Americans of African heritage have had the hardest time assimilating, and it's not the fault of any hyphen. Things were generally more hostile when we were called black, Negro, colored and worse. Indeed, it hasn't even been 25 years since the Rev. Jesse Jackson convened a news conference and declared that the people formerly known as black preferred "African American."

Whether Jackson was right or wrong is irrelevant. The point here is that no matter what black people have called themselves or have been called by others, our history is one of persistent ostracism and, yes, optimism. We've generally maintained a belief that rejection of us will diminish, even as it's diminished for other Americans more quickly.

Though Jindal uses his own biography as proof of America's greatness, he seems blissfully unaware that immigrants from India, as his parents were, were allowed to integrate into the American mainstream in ways the descendants of the slaves were not. Still, Jindal made it even easier for people to accept him, deciding that he'd rather be called Bobby—like the character from "The Brady Bunch"—than Piyush, the name his parents gave him.

I support a person's right to choose his name, whether it's as defiant as Cassius Clay becoming Muhammad Ali or as ignorant as Chad Johnson becoming Ochocinco. The governor can do what he wants. But I dream of an America where such a rejection of oneself isn't necessary, an America where a Piyush doesn't have to become a Bobby to belong.

YEARS WILL NEVER STEAL MOTHER'S MEMORY

DECEMBER 25, 2013

That last Christmas, my mother sat with a pair of scissors, a stack of plain white envelopes and sheets of family portraits taken in spring 2006. She cut out the individual pictures carefully and used her textbook penmanship to write the names of my dad's siblings, nieces and nephews on the envelopes. Later that day at my grandmother's house, while most of the family was absorbed with figuring out who had pulled whose name, my mother passed out her envelopes. She was all smiles that day. Except for those moments when she doubled over in pain.

The January before, she had been chatting with her oncologist when she saw that he had stopped talking and was staring at her. "Oh," she said, "you must be noticing that my eyes are yellow."

At an MLK holiday event her brother-in-law had hosted, she told her doctor, family had said the same thing, that her eyes were yellow. But those relatives didn't know what the oncologist did, that the jaundice was a sign of big trouble, that it contradicted the diagnostic exams that had pointed toward a breast cancer in remission. She had had plans that day, she told me on the phone. After her checkup at the oncologist, she had intended to browse in Belk's department store and eat at Captain D's. But the doctor had put her in the hospital. That's where she was when we talked.

There's no shortage of inspirational posters and greeting cards, motivational speakers and Facebook posts advising us to live each day as if it were our last. But if you've been told that your mother's breast cancer has broken loose and can't be cured, you may discover that imagining each holiday as the last with her isn't as sentimental as the inspirational industrial complex makes it out to be. You might be so worried it's the last, you can't stay in the moment.

That last Christmas, nobody said anything like, "This is the last Christmas," and yet, my mother's decision to distribute three-year-old pictures is pretty good evidence that she knew. She had married my father 37 years before and was a beloved sister, daughter and aunt. So her membership in the family was well established. Still, her choice to distribute pictures seemed to express a fear that she might otherwise slip from our memory.

I know well the fear of being forgotten—even now, with a byline and a picture that are published regularly. I had attributed it to that time in high school when I called a girl to confirm our big date the next night, and she said, "Oh, I forgot about you." But maybe the fear of being forgotten is more genetic than I realized. Maybe such worry is one of my mother's many gifts to me.

As it turns out, on that last Christmas, family pictures became sort of a theme. All the family that showed up—and I'd guess there were about five dozen of us—caravanned over to Hopewell Missionary Baptist Church, a building wide enough to get all of us in the picture.

After the group shot, the photographer took portraits of our individual families. And there we are again: my mom and dad, my sister and I and, for the first time in a family portrait, my wife, Kelly.

Mom's eyes are bright and white in that photo, but there's something off about her skin. She had had the complexion of the meat of a pecan, but now she was as dark as the shell. There's something else about the portrait that says she's sick, something other than the short-haired wig atop her head. I can't convey what that something else is. But when I reach for something to show my daughter what her grandmother looked like, I'll move past the photo taken that last Christmas.

Maybe that's why on a Christmas Day when we were taking family portraits, she distributed older portraits as gifts. The pictures put in envelopes were taken a year before the cancer diagnosis, back when she could still be called pretty. And what woman doesn't want to be remembered at her best?

I would see her again after Christmas, but it would be in a hospital, never again at home. My wife remembers that at the end of that Christmas visit, my mom walked us to the door and hugged us especially tight.

SHAME ON RAY NAGIN FOR PUTTING HIS FAMILY THROUGH THIS

Moments before the opening arguments in the trial of the New Orleans police accused of the post-Katrina killing of unarmed pedestrians on Danziger Bridge, one of the defendants looked over his shoulder and made eye contact with his family. Prosecutors were looking to separate that man and his co-defendants from their families for what might as well be called forever, and the look in his eyes was pleading, desperate, anxious. And at that moment, I imagined myself being forever separated from my family and was overcome by a deep sadness.

It's not supposed to be that way, is it? We are supposed to maintain a binary view of the world: good people, bad people. The good folks and their families are worthy of our empathy; the bad folks and their families are not. Well, sue me for not following the script. As I sat in a federal courtroom Monday before closing arguments in the trial for former New Orleans Mayor Ray Nagin, I ached for his family: his mother and father, his wife, Seletha.

During his initial campaign for mayor in 2002, Nagin made sure we all knew that he was born in Charity Hospital and that his father, Clarence Ray Nagin Sr., had often worked two jobs to support their family. One of those jobs the elder Nagin had? Janitor at New Orleans City Hall. Imagine what it must be like to see your son take complete charge of the building you used to sweep, take complete charge of the city in which you struggled to make a living. I can't imagine the magnitude of such pride.

Nor can I imagine what comes later: seeing that son standing in federal court as a defendant, hearing 12 jurors all say that yes, they agree, that Junior is guilty of 20 of the 21 charges made against him. How does Daedalus feel when he sees his son Icarus fly toward the sun just to crash back down into the sea?

Back in 1998, after a St. Tammany Parish jury found Jessie Hoffman guilty of kidnapping, robbing, raping and murdering Molly Elliot, his grandmother took the stand. The old woman was a diabetic, and testimony had revealed that Hoffman had been the grandchild who was gentle enough, patient enough, concerned enough to inject her daily with insulin. Penalty phase witnesses are expected to acknowledge the defendant's guilt as they plead for mercy, but Hoffman's grandmother didn't. "He was the best one. I raised him. He just ain't the kind. He got too much good in him to do something like that." She rested her forehead on the crook of her walking stick and wept.

Prosecutors and some of Elliot's family told me during the trial that they appreciated how fair my coverage had been. So my empathy for the defendant's family didn't result in stories that were any less concerned for the victim and her family. But I saw that old lady's testimony in my sleep. Her argument that a murderer such as Hoffman was good revealed something powerful about our capacity to love, about our loyalty to those people who have been kind to us.

If I could feel the pain of an officer accused of mowing down unarmed pedestrians after Katrina and conspiring to cover it up, if I could feel the pain of a grandmother crying for a man destined for death row, it shouldn't be surprising that I ache for Nagin's family as they brace themselves to be separated from him. Even when he was flying high, Nagin's wife, Seletha, never seemed comfortable with the public gaze. Though never impolite, the shy Seletha Nagin seemed to be making public appearances grudgingly, like she'd rather be somewhere else—by herself.

So imagine what she must have been feeling Wednesday, having first had to tell their son Jeremy on the phone that his father had been found guilty and then walking out into a scrum of photographers documenting the scene.

I'm just as upset as any other New Orleanian that Nagin sold his office and that a man as talented as he is would disgrace himself and hold our city up for ridicule. Despite his humble beginnings, he had made a great rise and was making a good deal of money before he became mayor. He traded that money for power. Then he decided that he still wanted the money, too.

We are all justified in being angry at Nagin for that. But I find myself just as angry at him for putting his family through this ordeal.

REMEMBERING AND RELEASING THE PAIN OF SLAVERY

JULY 9, 2014

While sitting on the sunlit cobblestones of Congo Square on Saturday morning, I couldn't help but wonder what gatherings at that sacred space must have looked like, must have sounded like, must have felt like, for long-ago captives who looked like me. Were those who had been held in the bellies of slave ships thankful that they had survived the torturous journey across the Atlantic Ocean, or were they envious of those who died and were fed to the sharks?

Were they bewildered and confused by the different African languages competing for attention at this square, or were they able to derive some small comfort that those languages sounded more like home than the European languages their oppressors were forcing into their mouths?

What messages would the enslaved have sent to their loved ones in their villages back home? If they could have spoken to future generations, what would they have said?

So much is unknown: languages, villages, religion, culture, occupations, social status. The people gathered at Congo Square Saturday morning were there out of respect for what we do know: Millions died in the Middle Passage, and even those who survived may have wished they hadn't.

The Swahili word used to describe the Middle Passage and the enslavement of Africans is "Maafa," meaning "great tragedy." We know that captives were worked unmercifully, even till death. We know that they were flogged and branded and raped and forcibly bred.

But in addition to all the horrible things we do know, there's the sorrow that comes from all the things we don't: origins, genealogy, names.

The historian Henry Louis Gates Jr. has described it as "that great abyss in our shared history: the void of slavery wherein the overwhelming percentage of our ancestors cease to exist as human beings, much less citizens, and indeed have no names that the legal system was bound to honor or acknowledge. They were just property, plain and simple."

But we remember them. Even if we don't know the names we should call. Even if we don't know the languages from which their names were derived, we remember them. It is necessary that we do.

Hence the 7 a.m. gathering at Congo Square on Saturday morning for the 14th Annual Maafa Commemoration. The remembrance was organized by the Ashé Cultural Arts Center in Central City.

Those in attendance varied in age. There were Christians, Muslims, Buddhists, Yoruba and others. There were people from different ethnicities and cultures and continents. That might seem like a recipe for disharmony and discord and tension. And yet, there was unity. Ifaseyi Sable Bamigbala Apetebi, a Yoruba priestess, used the following words in her invocation: "May the spirit of divine communication deliver all of our messages, whether spoken, whether thought, or laying at rest in our hearts. In this realm of the physical. And in the realm of the metaphysical. In this lifetime. And in any lifetime that we are blessed to have in the hereafter. For this generation. And for all the generations to come, may we have the blessings. Ashé."

On Tuesday morning, I asked Freddi Williams Evans, author of "Congo Square: African Roots in New Orleans," to tell me how Saturday morning's Maafa commemoration program compared with gatherings at Congo Square during the slavery era. She pointed out multiple similarities. Enslaved Africans who were allowed to go to Congo Square on Sundays would have been confronted by multiple African languages that they would not have necessarily understood. They would have interacted with others who didn't necessarily share their religious practices. And yet, they would have heard music—drums especially—that reminded them of home and allowed them to dance as one.

They would have come to Congo Square not only to buy and sell at that marketplace, Evans said, but they also would have come seeking some solace for their pain: the pain of displacement, the pain of the lash, the pain of having their families torn apart.

The Rev. Maurice Nutt, the director of Xavier University's Institute for Black Catholic Studies, in his litany addressed the pain that was not only experienced by those who were enslaved but also the pain that is still being experienced by their descendants. So as he verbally catalogued that pain, he prompted the people to say, "Heal us!"

Healing is as necessary as remembering. Carol Bebelle, the executive director of the Ashé Cultural Arts Center, said Saturday that the ancestors who endured the Maafa, who suffered under the torment of slavery, didn't struggle to survive just so we would be suffering still. It dishonors them, she said, to not work to free ourselves of the pain. "The past we inherit," Bebelle said. "The future we create."

WAS THERE SOMETHING IN RAY NAGIN THE CANDIDATE WE SHOULD HAVE NOTICED?

JULY 10, 2014

People in other places ask themselves if the chicken or the egg came first, but when Louisianans wave goodbye to public officials headed to jail, we are often left asking ourselves: Which came first? The appetite for corruption or the election to public office? That question was on my mind as I stood in line outside U.S. District Judge Ginger Berrigan's courtroom Wednesday morning. Ray Nagin, former mayor of New Orleans, was about to be sentenced. It was inconceivable to me in 2002 that I would ever be at a courthouse where Nagin would be sent off to prison.

I imagine that in the year that he was elected, it was inconceivable even to Nagin's enemies that he would eventually find himself standing before a federal judge with 20 felonies on his record. Richard Pennington, then the New Orleans police superintendent who bungled his mayoral election campaign, had said that Nagin's maneuvering to get a no-bid rental car concession at the airport "sickens me to my core." But even Pennington wasn't accusing Nagin of breaking the law—or any rules for that matter. Pennington's hyperbole came across as pure desperation, and it caused people who had had a great deal of respect for the police chief to laugh at and mock him.

Who would have guessed then that Nagin really would engage in a series of activities that—if not exactly sickening—were wholly despicable and wholly criminal, an abdication of his duties as the city's top official? Soon after he took office, he helped turn his alleged intolerance for corruption into the grandest theater: having low-level taxi cab drivers and brake-tag inspectors roused out of bed and perp walked, having then Utilities Department Director Lillian Regan publicly fired—in front of TV cameras.

Call me gullible. Call me too easily impressed. But I believed that any mayor who authorized such a strong response to government misdemeanors would never himself be caught in shenanigans. So did that shock-and-awe campaign, the opening salvo in what he called a "battle for the soul of New Orleans," really reflect what was then Nagin's intolerance for public corruption? Or was it a charade presented by a mayor who guessed that we would pay less attention to scrutinizing him if he took such a hardline approach?

Was Nagin plotting to do wrong when he campaigned for office, when he was sworn in, when he was announcing a war against corruption? Or did something happen subsequently that convinced him it was OK for him to use his office for his own personal gain and that it was OK to try to set up his sons with a coveted contract doing work for Home Depot?

Was there something we voters should have noticed in candidate Ray Nagin that could have spared us the great embarrassment of having a mayor sentenced to prison? Or is great power a carcinogen that leaves most who inhale it afflicted with arrogance and greed?

After Wednesday's proceedings were over and Judge Berrigan had shown mercy by imposing a sentence that was half as much as prosecutors wanted, Nagin reminded the public that arrogance and greed aren't the only vices plaguing him. His persecution complex persists.

"For some reason," he told WDSU-TV Wednesday, "some of the stances I took after Katrina did not sit well with some very powerful people, and I paid the price."

While Nagin did catch heat—and catch hate—for saying that a city that had been predominantly black before the storm would again be "chocolate at the end of the day," I hope he's not suggesting that said remark amounted to a "stance." One would be hard-pressed to name a single stance Nagin took after Hurricane Katrina—unless you count the stance he took against the "chocolate" folks in Central City who were negotiating for higher wages from a proposed Home Depot.

Nagin opposed them, and instead the company chose the mayor's two sons as contractors for granite countertop installations.

People convinced that "chocolate city" was a stance, that it represented a plan of Nagin's to help displaced black people regain a foothold in New Orleans, are as mistaken as those of us who thought the 2002 parade of taxi drivers and brake-tag inspectors signaled a new day of integrity.

Besides, Nagin wasn't indicted, convicted and sentenced for anything he said. He's headed to prison for things he did. Which is ironic when you remember how opposed he seemed to doing anything his whole second term.

Nagin's 2006 re-election disappointed many who didn't think he was up to the task. But I doubt that even his opponents then thought he was up to dirt.

STOP GAP

Young black men should count on unfair interactions with police

OCTOBER 15, 2014

Hundreds of young black men gathered in the gymnasium at Dillard University on Monday morning to talk to local law enforcement officials about how they might survive their inevitable interactions with the police. But those teenagers may have left Dillard confused. They got a steady dose of advice to get an education and to stay well groomed and presentable from educated, well-groomed and presentable black men who shared their own stories about being wrongly suspected by the police.

At the start of the program, the black men on the dais gave the teenagers every reason to believe that— no matter what they do or who they are—they should count on being stopped. Criminal Court Judge Benedict Willard, who comes from a large, well-known New Orleans family, said he had already graduated college when New Orleans officers, casting a net for drug users, forced him to the ground and separated his shoulder.

"When they went into my wallet," the judge said, they "found out my last name, fortunately, was Willard. But I got a problem with the fact that if my last name was not Willard, a different outcome would have taken place."

U.S. Attorney Kenneth Polite, a Harvard graduate, said police went through his pockets after they pulled over a car with him and other Harvard and Tufts students for "the proverbial broken taillight." Polite said he's also been "stopped and detained for wearing too much red." That's a color of his college fraternity, he said, but police suspected him of gang affiliation.

"Everybody has stories about being stopped for the color of our skin or being stopped for reasons we don't know." That statement wasn't made by one of the teenagers but by Michael Harrison, interim superintendent of the New Orleans Police Department.

Sheriff Marlin Gusman, who went to Wharton, the business school at the University of Pennsylvania, said, "The U.S. attorney talked about being stopped. I've been stopped before. I've been stopped several times. I remember one time I was stopped. I was in college. I think the only thing that saved me was that I pulled out my college ID."

Got it? There were four black male public officials on the stage, and each of the four had a story about being wrongly suspected of something. Not long after those testimonials, a student from St. Augustine High School asked, "What makes a person look suspicious?"

Gusman praised that teenager for not looking suspicious himself, for being well groomed and for being dressed presentably. He was not, Gusman noted, walking around with sagging pants. Gusman's response was at odds with what he had already said about needing a college ID to satisfy an officer. It was also at odds with what he said next: "I've been stopped as an adult," he said, "when I was the city's chief administrative officer."

We know that when Gusman was then-Mayor Marc
Morial's CAO, he wasn't sagging his pants. That didn't
stop him from being stopped, though.

This is what must have confused the teenagers. The
adults were telling them stories of unfair stops while
implying that they could prevent themselves from being unfairly stopped.

Judge Willard said most of the defendants he sees in
court are not educated. So he encouraged Monday's
students—most were from St. Aug with some from
Lake Area High School—to stay in school. Willard
guessed that if he asked them if they knew somebody
who'd been arrested, almost all would say yes. But that
wouldn't be true at Newman, he said.

So a black boy who is educated will be treated dif-
ferently than a white boy who is educated. The cops
may rough him up so bad that his shoulder separates.
It's never bad advice to promote education, but Willard's own story about being manhandled by the police
suggests that it won't necessarily matter to police who
reflexively suspect black men of wrongdoing.

To the student who asked what makes a person
look suspicious, Superintendent Harrison said, "We
look at suspicious behavior, not how you're dressed or
how you're groomed, per se." Well, they should. In his
opening remarks, Polite said the New Orleans Police
Department has led the country in the rate of credible
allegations of police abuse.

Polite told the students to do like he used to do: keep
with them a card that reminds them of their rights
when they're stopped.

"You're not going to be able to address police conduct
right there on the street," he said. "Get yourself out of

that incident if you believe that police conduct is actually at play."

Sound advice. But if students came to Dillard expecting to learn how to get the police to ignore them altogether, surely they left disappointed.

NEW ORLEANS SLAVE-TRADE EXHIBIT DISPLAYS THE PAIN OF BEING PURCHASED WHILE HUMAN

MARCH 23, 2015

On the second floor of "Purchased Lives," an exhibit at The Historic New Orleans Collection, there is a wall of classified ads that were placed after slavery was illegal by the loved ones of those who may have been bought and sold in New Orleans.

That wall of reproduced and magnified newspaper ads may be the most evocative display in what is a uniformly powerful exhibit. Over and over again, those ads remind the person taking in the exhibit that the people who were bought and sold here were just that: people.

They were loved.

They were missed.

Freedom had come, but how much good was that freedom if it didn't bring families back together, if it didn't reunite husbands to their wives, mothers and fathers to their sold-off children?

And so they wrote to the editors of newspapers that circulated throughout the South, including New Orleans. Did anybody know the whereabouts of Sally, who used to belong to a Mr. Smith? Had anybody seen John, who used to belong to a man named Williams?

Those ads were almost always placed in vain. Erin Greenwald, the curator of "Purchased Lives," said Thursday that she knows of one instance—a single, solitary instance—of a person who placed a newspaper ad later contacting the editor to report that it had led to their loved one being found.

Slavery routinely tore apart families, and if the near-zero success rate of the newspaper ads is any indication, for many of those families, the rupture was permanent.

Greenwald said the woman in charge of that part of the exhibit "was kind of a mess" as she was putting all those ads together. Who wouldn't be? The ads transform the lost ones from slaves into family members. No longer are those who were in bondage part of a nameless black mass. They are mother, brother, nephew, daughter. They are people. They always were people, despite their previous designation as property.

More human beings were bought and sold in New Orleans than in any other place in America. And yet, the city's outsized role in that despicable trade was "a subject we have not addressed," Greenwald said.

Slavery helped make New Orleans incredibly rich. How big of an industry was it? "It was huge!" Greenwald said. "Huge!" Some banks in the city were founded primarily to extend credit to slavers. You know, in the likelihood that you'd need a mortgage to buy a person. Insurance companies formed to provide policies on that human property and to cover any damage they might suffer during shipment. Uprisings excluded.

And there was a pretty stiff sales tax on a person, so the government profited handsomely.

I asked Greenwald, "Has New Orleans ever been as wealthy as it was when people were being put up for sale?"

She shook her head. "No," she said, "not even with the oil boom."

Importing enslaved Africans into the country became a crime in 1808. The transatlantic trade was stopped. So the legal slave trade became a domestic affair, with 1 million enslaved people being shipped from the upper South to the lower South between 1808 and abolition. Many came through New Orleans.

"We had the largest volume of individual men, women and children sold here in the city of any Southern city in the antebellum period, which means any city in the United States, not just the South."

We've all heard the phrase, "Better the devil you know than the devil you don't know." As Greenwald led me through the exhibit, it occurred to me that there is no better example of that thinking than people running off when they feared they would soon be sold.

Running away, of course, was likely to lead to the same separation from family as being sold would have. And yet, people were willing to run. So it must have been that they feared the unknown of a new owner more than the certain pain of being separated from their loved ones.

"Unlike many cities," Greenwald said, "the sales and purchases of human beings did not take place in one single market structure." Pointing to a 19th century map of New Orleans, she said, "Purchases and sales took place all over the city."

Abolitionist iconography almost always shows those human beings being sold at auction, Greenwald said, and though there were auctions, people were also transferred as property in bankruptcy proceedings and sheriff's sales.

She said, "We have an example of an individual man being raffled off in a lottery."

AFTER KATRINA, NEW ORLEANIANS NEEDED HELP TO FIND LOVED ONES

MARCH 29, 2015

As Hurricane Katrina moved toward the Louisiana coastline and threatened to submerge New Orleans, Vincent Sylvain, a former official in the Marc Morial administration, considered staying put. He was doing some contract work for Sheriff Marlin Gusman, Sylvain said by phone Thursday, and he thought he could be of help if he stayed.

"I almost felt guilty leaving the city," he said.

But there are an untold number of people who are thankful that Sylvain left the city for a hotel room in Port Arthur, Texas. Because by getting out of the city, Sylvain was able to tend to his website, The New Orleans Agenda. Created in 2002 to promote the campaigns of Sylvain's political clients, it soon became, Sylvain said, a way of getting immediate news to readers who didn't want to wait for the next issue of their favorite black newspaper.

After Katrina scattered New Orleanians across the country, Sylvain's website took on a new purpose: connecting the scattered to one another. People who didn't know where their loved ones were or knew their loved ones were worried about them—they went to Sylvain's website to ask, "Where are you?" or to say, "This is where I am."

Sylvain said he had between 10,000 and 12,000 sub-scribers to his site before the disaster and that after-ward that number swelled to about 70,000. Imagine asking on a site with that much traffic, "Do you know where my loved one is?"

Just about everybody who had a mobile phone with a 504 number had trouble placing and receiving calls that Katrina week. But not Sylvain. "I don't know how," he said, "but my phone never stopped working. When folks found out they could contact me by telephone, they would call me to relay a message to somebody they couldn't call."

And those who could find an Internet connection started sending Sylvain their information and asking about their loved ones.

That's what Janice Brown did. She and her family rode out the storm at the Holiday Inn on Loyola Av-enue where her brother worked. They left her broth-er at the hotel that Monday and eventually arrived at Brown's apartment on Ninth Street.

"A little after midnight," she said Friday, "the police came into our neighborhood and said, 'You all have to get out, there's water coming into the city.'"

But what about her brother?

"I couldn't use my phone," Brown said. "It was charged, but I couldn't use my phone."

It was in Shreveport, Brown said, that she "started getting email from Vincent." In fact, she said, "My email was filled with his email of people looking for people." So she gave it a try. Had anybody seen her brother?

And soon she had an answer. "Your brother is still at the hotel," somebody responded, "and he's trying to call you."

Brown lives in Austin, Texas now. I found her through Twitter on Friday morning. I asked if anybody had used Sylvain's site to connect with family after Katrina, and she responded, "Yes, and family who couldn't find US, found us through him!" Though we'd never met, our phone conversation revealed why Sylvain's site connected people as well as it did.

"The other person I was looking for," Brown said, "was (jazz musician) Harold Battiste because I worked with him, and I was really concerned about him. Somebody responded that Harold was fine."

"Harold goes to my church," I said.

"Oh," she said, "you go to Christian Unity Baptist Church."

Then Brown mentioned the names of other friends she had tracked down through Sylvain's site, and I knew most of them, too.

"He was incredibly helpful," Brown said of Sylvain. "Nobody helped in New Orleans like he did."

Of course, he wouldn't have been able to help as much if people weren't online. "Katrina forced New Orleanians to become more familiar with the Internet," Sylvain said. "People discovered they could apply to FEMA and other government agencies more quickly if they went online." And when they realized it was a more reliable way to reach loved ones, many senior citizens started texting or emailing.

Not just seniors. Though I text frequently now, I never had before Katrina.

"It was a massive movement that kind of forced New Orleans to be on a higher level of technology," Sylvain said.

Before our interview Sylvain looked at messages that passed through his site in 2005. "It's almost like reliving the whole experience all over again," he said.

At one point he ran out of space on his server and had to delete some items. Even so, "I've got thousands, thousands of communications thanking me for helping find individuals."

JENA 6 DEFENDANT HEADS TO LAW SCHOOL

APRIL 10, 2015

Louisiana almost threw Theo Shaw away. This state—which discards black men and boys like pecan shells, like potato peels and coffee grounds—nearly added Shaw to its refuse pile, to its towering heap of incarcerated bodies.

A Louisiana prosecutor had Shaw charged with attempted murder, alleging that he participated in an attack at Jena High School, a high school so simmering with racial tension that three white students there had hung a noose from a tree.

Shaw and the other young black men who became known as the Jena 6 were presented to the world as the epitome of savagery. They needed to be charged with attempted murder for sending a white schoolmate to the emergency room. It didn't matter that he was soon discharged or that he was feeling well enough to attend a school event the next night. The Jena 6 needed to be taught a lesson. They needed to be thrown away.

But in September 2007, several thousand people from across the country converged in Jena and expressed outrage at Louisiana's attempt to permanently ruin the young men's lives. Shaw, whose inability to post bail had left him in jail seven months, was eventually released. Though he insists that he played no role in the attack on the student, in court Shaw pleaded no contest to misdemeanor simple battery.

Almost eight years after that massive march in Jena, Shaw is breaking free of Louisiana. He will enroll this fall at the School of Law at the University of Washington. That law school, which U.S. News & World Report puts in the country's top 30, has chosen Shaw as one of the incoming class's five William H. Gates Public Service Law Scholars. It's a full scholarship, covering tuition, books and even some money for room and board and incidental expenses.

"You have already shown yourself to be a person of commitment and drive," the letter congratulating Shaw reads. "Your participation as a Gates Scholar will help us continue to build our law school community, and will also help in making our world a better place."

We wouldn't be talking about Shaw's potential to improve the world if he were still in prison. And he'd probably be in prison without that mobilization on behalf of the Jena 6. Those protesters didn't know Shaw personally. They may not have even been able to call his name, but, he said Monday, "They knew me, they knew us, through history."

It's a history that includes young black boys being thrown away as trash. It's a history that's bigger than Louisiana's.

Shaw said in a May 2014 interview that he was so unconcerned with school that he thinks he was ranked dead last in his senior class. Black, poor, uneducated and male in Louisiana. What better candidate for being thrown away like trash?

All the more reason, perhaps, that the state of Louisiana, in the form of LaSalle Parish District Attorney J. Reed Walters, had no qualms about throwing Shaw away.

It was widely reported that before the incident leading to Shaw's arrest, but while racial tensions at Jena were simmering, Walters warned a Jena High assembly that he could change their lives "with the stroke of a pen."

With Shaw and the others, he certainly tried.

"I was forced to be hopeful," Shaw said Monday about his seven months in jail. "To not be hopeful would be to give into their belief of who I was."

And who is Theo Shaw, really?

When I asked Rob McDuff, Shaw's mentor and the attorney who helped free him from jail, he answered, "Theo has a kind and gentle spirit. He is engaging and makes friends easily. He is extremely curious and reads widely. He thinks before he speaks (which is too rare in this world), and when he does speak, he is very clear and insightful. He is smart and is committed to helping people who have been dealt a bad hand in life."

If convicted as originally charged, Shaw could have been imprisoned for 50 years.

Though he refused to believe he was as bad as the district attorney said, it took Shaw time to believe that he was as good as his supporters were telling him.

"I had to believe in their belief in me till mine kicked in," he said. Now a law school in Seattle is expressing a similar belief.

"For a school to believe in you so much that they would just cover everything?" Shaw said. "I'm profoundly grateful."

It's a gratitude that includes knowing that he could have been sentenced to decades as some kind of monster.

And if he had been thrown away, we never would
have known just how wrong that was.

STATUE OF LEE AN ISSUE FOR N.O.

Mayor concerned how symbol fits in city's future

JUNE 24, 2015

Nikki Haley, governor of South Carolina, reversed course Monday and said she thinks the Confederate battle flag should be removed from its place of prominence on the grounds of the state capitol in Columbia. After Dylann Storm Roof, a 21-year-old white supremacist, killed nine people in a Charleston church Wednesday, the pressure to take down the flag became too much for Haley to fight.

That flag, a symbol of hate and racism, doesn't fly over any government offices in New Orleans. But we still have many monuments to the Confederacy.

The most prominent one is certainly the statue to Confederate Gen. Robert E. Lee that towers over Lee Circle. Mayor Mitch Landrieu has been talking about whether the Lee monument ought to have a future as New Orleans approaches its 300th birthday.

Here's what Landrieu's office said Monday afternoon: "Mayor Landrieu has discussed with 2018 Tricentennial Commission members how we can appropriately recognize our 300-year history as a city while also looking to the future and helping New Orleans become the city we always knew she could be. Part of this process should include a close examination of the historical symbols throughout our city and what changes could be made as we approach 2018, including the Robert E. Lee statute in Lee Circle. These symbols say who we were in a particular time, but times change. Yet these symbols, statues, monuments, street names, and more—still influence who we are and how we are perceived by the world. Mayor Landrieu believes it is time to look at the symbols in this city to see if they still have relevance to our future."

It's good to see the use of the word "symbols" in that statement because it wouldn't be right to say that Robert E. Lee's statue is the only monument in New Orleans that's offensive.

I was not in New Orleans for the fight over the monument to the "White League," a group that killed 11 members of the integrated Metropolitan New Orleans Police Force on Canal Street. I didn't know what that monument near my office at One Canal Place and Audubon Aquarium was even about until April. That's when civil rights attorney Mary Howell said she thinks it's the only monument in the country that celebrates the killing of police officers.

"I think it's shameful," she said Monday.

Shawn Anglim, pastor of First Grace United Methodist, a church at the intersection of Canal Street and Jefferson Davis Parkway, thinks it's shameful that there's a statue to Confederate President Jefferson Davis in what he calls his front yard.

The killings in Charleston last week gave his opposition to the statue a new urgency, Anglim said from his office Monday. "You get used to trying to tell your children why it's not a big deal, but it is a big deal," he said. "It's a monument."

It's time for Jefferson Davis to go, Anglim said. "I'm not looking for a drawn-out government discussion. I'm looking for a welder."

Retired Marine Lt. Col. Rich Westmoreland, a new New Orleanian and a native Kentuckian, started a correspondence with me in May about the city's many monuments to the Confederacy. "I understand why the citizens of this city in the 1880s thought erecting a statue to General Lee was a good idea," he wrote. "But for the life of me I don't understand why it stands in the middle of any U.S. city in 2015."

Westmoreland, who said he's a descendant of Confederate officers, said Monday, "We're the U.S. before we're the South."

Well, we ought to be.

Last year Judge Calvin Johnson, retired from the Criminal District Court in Orleans Parish, talked about his hope to see a New Orleans statue for André Cailloux, who was born in slavery, bought his freedom and led an all-black group of Union soldiers at Port Hudson.

Not only is there no statue to Cailloux in New Orleans, there isn't one for anybody who fought for the Union.

According to composer Hannibal Lokumbe, who has lived on and off in New Orleans, he and sculptor John Scott were taking a walk once when they came across the Jefferson Davis statue. Lokumbe says Scott, who died in 2007, said, "Every time I see this statue I get sick to my stomach." They came up with their own personal and pungent protest, Lokumbe said. At the first full moon of every month, they would meet at the statue of Jefferson Davis and pee on it.

YOU CAN'T GO HOME AGAIN
A decade later, a neighborhood is transformed

AUGUST 30, 2015

Years after the storm, as a weary traveler on the Road Home, I sold my house on Crescent Street to the state of Louisiana. I could have rebuilt it, but I didn't. I had multiple reasons for cutting ties to the property. First and foremost, I didn't want a frontier experience. I didn't want to risk rebuilding on a block I wasn't sure would recover.

Second, I didn't feel an emotional attachment to the house. I'd bought it in January 2004. It was inundated with water in August 2005. That was not enough time, I told myself, to be sentimental about it. So here, Louisiana, take it.

As a previous column revealed, I felt different in January 2010 as I watched a work crew demolishing the house. I felt like the Delta blues genius Son House, who, in the voice of a man who sees his lover buried, sings, "I didn't know I loved her till they let her down."

Setting aside the six weeks I spent sleeping in my cousin's guest room in Baton Rouge, I've lived in three other houses since leaving Crescent Street. Still, whenever I can, I drive past my old property to see what's happened to it and the surrounding neighborhood.

As the 10th anniversary of Hurricane Katrina approached, I grew increasingly curious about the tall yellow house that stands where my blue bungalow did. Who bought the property and why? What attracted them there, and what do they think about their choice?

Contractor Kurt Tatje graduated from Holy Cross High School, which, after its Lower 9th Ward campus was flooded, was looking to move to an area bordered by Crescent Street. His wife, Natalie Tatje, graduated from Cabrini High School. That school's mascot is the Crescent. So the decision to search for property on Crescent Street was partially "from the gut," Natalie Tatje said Friday.

But the husband and wife weren't guided entirely by sentimentality. "We felt like we could make it work," she said. They believed Holy Cross would be built nearby, but even if that didn't happen, she said, "We just felt like (the neighborhood) would come back."

Was it a good investment?

"Absolutely," she said. "Without a doubt."

Tatje and her husband live in LaPlace and rent the house they built on my old lot. They also own a house two doors down from my old property. Kurt Tatje's sister, Susan, lives there.

She welcomed me into her home Thursday evening to talk about what the neighborhood is like 10 years after it sat in eight feet of water.

"It was like a frontier out here" when she arrived in 2009, Susan Tatje said. But now she sees expectant couples walking in the evenings and families pushing strollers.

As NOLA.com's "Yat Map" has revealed, not everybody who lives in a neighborhood agrees on what it is called. When I lived on Crescent Street, I said I lived in Gentilly. Some call it Oak Park because that's the name of the neighborhood association. But there's a new name gaining currency, and some people on the Yat Map have used it.

"Apparently we're being called Lakeview East now," Susan Tatje said.

She has nothing against Lakeview. She lived at Memphis and Filmore when the 17th Street Canal failure flooded the house with 11 feet of water. Even so, she said, "We don't really want to be Lakeview."

Alden McDonald, president and CEO of Liberty Bank, said earlier this month that New Orleans has almost no workforce housing. But that's all my neighborhood was around me when I lived in Gentilly. I bought my house for $147,000.

Susan Tatje said Thursday that after the storm she remembers lots near Crescent Street going for $15,000 to $20,000. But Realtor.com now lists four vacant lots in the area for $90,000 to $129,000.

After leaving Susan Tatje's home, I saw 73-year-old Larry Bonds, the owner of a lawn-care business, outside his house on Mithra Street. "Hey, Mr. Larry!" I said.

"Hey, Jarvis!"

It felt good seeing him again. His hands were covered with oil, though. So we bumped the backs of our hands instead of shaking them.

"This neighborhood is moving!" he said. Moving too fast for some people, it seems.

He nodded. It's filling up with doctors, lawyers, he said. "We got five engineers." He pointed to a house in the next block that he said sold for $395,000 after the owner asked $410,000.

"In this neighborhood?!"

"Yeah," he nodded. "Yeah."

"I can't remember the last time a black person bought around here," he said, describing the buyers as mostly young and white. "I think they done out-priced us."

A HEARTBREAKING HISTORY
Little is left after tornado lifts away roof of house
Wind and water destroy two homes, 10 years apart

DECEMBER 30, 2015

Ten years after a devastating flood inundated the first house I bought in New Orleans, an unusually powerful and unusually long-lasting tornado ripped apart the only house my parents ever bought.

They moved into their new house on Old Highway 4 West outside Holly Springs, Mississippi when I was 4.

When I was 5, I graduated from the day care at Rust College. I sat for a photo wearing a white cap and gown and a white tassel. My infant sister, wearing a red dress, was placed on my lap. As I was picking through the rubble Saturday afternoon, I found that picture. The wall on which it hung was no more. It was no longer in a frame. It lay on a pile of debris in what used to be the den, now open and exposed to the sky.

I spent hours on that pile of rubble Saturday looking for any little bit of something we could salvage. I wanted the bedroom furniture that belonged to my great-grandparents. I found the headboard, but the frame of the bed was buried, and the dresser had a brick wall angled across it. A Victrola that belonged to that same set of great-grandparents was pinned down by another brick wall.

One of my father's co-workers showed up with his wife to help us look for things. Many yards away from our house, where my folks used to grow cabbage and purple hull peas and watermelons, that co-worker's wife found a huge black Bible that I figured had belonged to my maternal grandmother. The funeral program of one of her sisters was tucked into the pages. So was a snapshot of my grandmother's second husband.

My mother passed away almost six years ago. These items were passed down through the generations to her. I wanted to save them for her, but with the weight of the bricks and the softening effect of the rain, we may not be able to restore them even after they're excavated from beneath the bricks.

Saturday evening, after I lay down to sleep in the guest room of an uncle's house, it occurred to me that I had not seen the roof of the destroyed house. Because I had seen photos of the damage before I made it to Mississippi, I knew that the tornado had torn the roof off. But it wasn't until hours after I'd left the scene of the destruction that I realized that I hadn't even seen a sign of the roof.

Not a single shingle.

I could understand a roof being torn up. I could understand a roof being torn off. But I couldn't make sense of it being wholly and completely gone.

Speaking of disbelief, Thursday morning on The Weather Channel, a reporter standing in another torn-apart house near Holly Springs said the tornado in question had stayed on the ground for 2 hours, 45 minutes and 150 miles. Investigators believe that tornado reached F3 intensity. That's between 158 and 206 miles per hour. By comparison, a Category 5 hurricane has a wind speed of 156 miles per hour or greater.

Though a wind that was believed to be more than 156 miles per hour ripped the roof off the house, the three people who were huddled inside emerged without a scratch. My sister, her boyfriend and their 2-year-old daughter balled themselves up in a bathtub. That tub—like every other fixture in the house—is now completely exposed to the sky.

A roof that blew away and three human beings who did not.

After my mother died, my family and I were going through old pictures, and I came across one of my dad when he was of courting age. I studied it for a long while because, to the best of my knowledge, it was the earliest photo I'd ever seen of him, probably the earliest photo that exists. I've never seen a photo of my father as a boy. I don't know exactly why that is. But I suspect that my grandparents, who had 11 children, didn't have much money to spend on getting pictures made.

I always thought that was a tragedy: the absence of photos chronicling my father's childhood.

Then Katrina happened, and just like that, all my high school yearbooks and all my college-age photos were gone.

So I pounced on the photo of me graduating from day care. It's part of the photographic record that I have in existence—despite two cataclysmic events that have come closing to wiping that record clean.

NUMBNESS . . . AFTER GUILTY PLEAS IN DANZIGER BRIDGE MASSACRE

APRIL 22, 2016

They did it. The New Orleans police officers accused of killing and maiming innocent people on the Danziger Bridge the Sunday after Hurricane Katrina? And accused of attempting to cover up their crimes by concocting a story that they were under attack? The same officers who were hailed as heroes when they arrived at the courthouse to face state charges? They did it.

In a federal courtroom Wednesday, Kenneth Bowen, Robert Gisevius, Robert Faulcon, Anthony Villavaso and Arthur Kaufman, all accused of crimes related to the Danziger Bridge massacre, stood up one by one and admitted what they've been denying for more than 10 years.

"Guilty," Bowen said.

"Guilty, your honor," said the rest.

Their admissions serve as rebuke to all the police apologists who showered them with praise and thought it ridiculous when Eddie Jordan, the former district attorney for Orleans Parish, wrote, "We cannot allow our police officers to shoot and kill our citizens without justification, like rabid dogs."

Those same officers stood and admitted Wednesday—that just like Jordan wrote in his December 2006 statement—they were without justification when they killed 40-year-old Ronald Madison and 17-year-old James Brissette.

And yet, their admissions provided none of the catharsis one might expect to accompany cops pleading guilty. On Wednesday, the U.S. government officially won its case against Bowen, Gisevius, Faulcon, Villavaso and Kaufman. But it was a victory that had the feel of defeat.

A jury found the men guilty after a trial in August 2011, but two years later U.S. District Judge Kurt Engelhardt said that misconduct on the part of prosecutors—"jiggery-pokery" is the word he used Wednesday—obligated him to give the officers a new trial. Seven judges on the 5th U.S. Circuit Court of Appeals disagreed with Engelhardt. But seven justices agreed. That tie preserved Engelhardt's ruling.

The guilty pleas that followed the appellate court's tie vote meant that Faulcon's sentence was reduced by 82 percent: from 65 years in prison to 12. Bowen's sentence was reduced by 75 percent: from 40 years in prison to 10. Ditto, Gisevius': from 40 years to 10. Kaufman's sentence was sliced in half: from 6 years to 3. Like Faulcon, Villavaso received an 82 percent sentence reduction. He had gotten 38 years; now he's sentenced to 7.

With the exception of Kaufman, all these defendants have been locked up since 2010, and all of them (Kaufman included) are being given credit for the time they've already served. So when the judge said he was sentencing Villavaso to seven years, everybody with elementary math skills could figure it out. That means Villavaso's coming home soon.

And the others not too far behind him.

None of Ronald Madison's relatives chose to speak at Wednesday's court hearing. Neither did Brissette's mother, Sherrell Johnson. Nobody spoke on behalf of Susan Bartholomew—whose right arm was blown off by the police on Sept. 4, 2005. Nobody spoke on behalf of any of the pedestrians who were harmed by the police. But Judge Engelhardt did say that the "consent of the surviving victims" played a critical role in his decision to accept the plea deals.

Other than saying that they were guilty and other than answering "yes, sir" and "no, sir" at the appropriate times, the defendants didn't say anything either—at least not for themselves. Attorney Eric Hessler, who represents Gisevius, faced the families in the courtroom and said his client "extends his sympathy" for the "tragic incident." Kaufman's attorney, Billy Gibbens, said, "We apologize" for the losses the families suffered.

Neither of those two apologies contained any hint of emotion. Each seemed more like a hollow gesture than a sincere expression of contrition.

Kaufman was the sergeant in charge of the Danziger investigation, who brought a gun from his house and said it had been fired at police on the bridge. He was attempting to frame Lance Madison. Not only did Madison lose his developmentally disabled brother on the bridge, but he was wrongly booked with attempting to murder police officers. Kaufman's attempt to frame him could have sent him to prison forever.

I looked over Wednesday to see how Madison was receiving the attorneys' apologies. His mouth was closed, but he looked to be clenching his teeth.

"I finally got what I wanted. Someone confessed," Johnson said.

The officers' admissions are important. I just wish there was going to be more time between those guilty admissions and those guilty officers returning home.

FROM THE STREETS TO YALE, A JOURNEY "BEYOND IMAGINATION"

MAY 25, 2016

When I connected with Troy Simon via Skype on May 19, I asked him how far removed he feels from New Orleans. Simon, who will be graduating from Bard College in New York on Saturday, said, "I don't think I'm too far removed from New Orleans, but I am a little removed." When he elaborated, though, it sounded like more than a little.

"It seems as if I have this double consciousness," Simon said, using the term that pioneering black scholar W.E.B. Du Bois used to describe the "twoness" that comes with being black and American. "Because sometimes I cannot relate to my family members on the level that I used to relate to them. It's really difficult for me to connect with them as opposed to connecting to people back at school because we're able to talk...and use highfalutin language in our daily conversations."

But it can also be hard connecting with some people at college whose lives of relative ease contrast with his life of grinding poverty.

There's this persistent American myth that black people find it uncool to be educated. That's not it. What black people find, way too often, is that their educations threaten to pull them away from their loved ones without making them feel at home at school. Simon's trying to fit in both places. "I was just like my family," he said. He's where he is today because of his family, and they and their opinions matter to him.

Simon hasn't always used highfalutin language. He was a functionally illiterate teenager who, when he wasn't selling weed or stealing copper, fastened caps to the bottom of his shoes and danced for tips in the French Quarter. During 2008's Carnival, he was pedaling toward Bourbon Street, his tapping shoes slung over his shoulder. That's when he biked past Sarah Bliss, who remembered teaching him in fifth grade. She called out to him. He stopped, and the tutoring Bliss offered put him on a path to literacy, graduation from Sci Academy and admission to college in upstate New York.

Four years after leaving New Orleans for New York, Simon will be leaving New York for New Haven, Connecticut, to study at Yale Divinity School.

When we walk through the French Quarter and see children dancing with caps on their shoes, it's doubtful that we imagine any of them as future scholars. It's more likely that we think of them as future drug addicts and prisoners. And that is what they could become if nobody takes an interest in them, Simon said. His success, he believes, "shows you that these kids are really talented and very smart, but they're not invested in as much as they should be invested in."

In 2012, when Simon completed the Urban League College Track program, he pulled on his tapping shoes and showed the audience what he used to do before he could read. Former President Bill Clinton, who spoke at the College Track graduation ceremony, expressed disbelief that Simon had no formal dance training. When we Skyped last week, Simon mentioned Clinton's surprised reaction to underscore his point that this city's children are full of potential.

"You just mentioned Bill Clinton," I said. "He's not the only president you've met."

Simon smiled, almost sheepishly. "No, he's not. President Barack Obama. I met him two years ago." He shook his head as if he's still struggling to believe it. In January 2014, Simon met the president and Michelle Obama at a College Opportunity Summit held at the Eisenhower Executive Office Building, next door to the White House. He introduced Michelle Obama at the event. There are photos of him posing for pictures with the Obamas. But the photo that gives me the most chills is the one that shows Simon speaking from a lectern affixed with the presidential seal.

What was meeting the Obamas like?

He shook his head some more. "Coming from an abandoned building, being marooned for Hurricane Katrina, tap dancing in the French Quarter, going to Bard College...and being illiterate, I mean, this experience seemed unreal to me.

"It would have been beyond my imagination in the halcyon days of my youth to see that moment come into existence."

Did you catch that? He used "halcyon" in a sentence. Just dropped it in there like nothing.

Simon may not talk like a New Orleans street kid, but he wants to use his degree from Yale to contribute to the city of his birth. "If I didn't have the educators, the teachers, the people in my life to come say, 'Hey, I believe in you,' I don't think I would be where I'm at today."

ALTON STERLING WAS JUST TRYING TO MAKE A LIVING

JULY 10, 2016

Though 37-year-old Alton Sterling joins a depressingly long list of black Americans whose deaths at the hands of police seemed unnecessary, he and 43-year-old Eric Garner are also on a list unto themselves.

Like Garner, who was selling loose cigarettes before New York police put him in a chokehold, Sterling was working his hustle when police accosted him. He was peddling CDs before Baton Rouge police shot him to death.

If you're black, chances are you've at least nodded at a hustle man: the man on the street hawking bunnies and bears and tinfoil balloons in advance of Valentine's Day; the man in the beauty shops selling everything from sweet potato pies to knockoff handbags; the man in the night club selling long-stem plastic roses.

Last month, at the Cleveland Cavaliers' victory parade, my wife took note of the street-level entrepreneurs who were selling shiny packets of Capri Sun for $2 a pop.

Don't laugh. You've paid more for water at a game.

Such a familiar presence is the hustle man that the 1990s sitcom "Martin," which was set in Detroit, had a character named just that: Hustle Man.

The hustle man can sometimes be a bother—I don't particularly care to buy my music in the Walgreens parking lot—but I figure most black folks respond to him with a shrug and a quote from that Tupac song "I Ain't Mad At Cha." Say, bruh, I may not be interested in Latimore's greatest hits, but I ain't mad at cha.

And, usually, there's no good reason to be mad at or afraid of the man hustling "loosies" or bootleg CDs. He's just trying to make a dollar—or maybe four or five.

Late Tuesday night, at the Triple S Food Mart where Baton Rouge police killed Sterling, a woman who had bought CDs from Sterling and was there protesting his homicide spoke to a reporter. "If he's out here at 12:30 at night selling CDs, he ain't rich," she said. "He's hustling. Getting money. Ain't nothing wrong with hustling."

Some people in that area of Baton Rouge knew Sterling simply as CD Man. The owner of the Triple S Food Mart apparently had no problem with his trade. Abdul Muflahi, who in interviews has referred to Sterling as a friend, said Sterling had sold CDs outside his store for a long time but became concerned when a friend with the same CD-selling hustle was robbed.

According to CNN, Tuesday morning's fatal episode was set in motion when a homeless man kept pestering Sterling for cash. I guess if you're the CD Man you can't pretend to be without money. According to CNN's law enforcement source, when the man wouldn't stop his begging, Sterling showed him his gun and said, "I told you to leave me alone." The man called 911 and said Sterling threatened him.

I'm not inclined to make the 911 caller's life any less important than Sterling's. If the 911 caller's report is true, then he was the victim of a crime. At the same time, it's easy to sympathize with Sterling—both in his decision to try to protect himself from being robbed and his apparent exasperation at a beggar's refusal to walk away.

As a convicted felon, Sterling didn't have the legal right to possess a firearm, but Muflahi suggests he had one because he thought it would keep him from being victimized. Though Muflahi insists that Sterling didn't so much as reach for his weapon, count on his possession of it to be used by police apologists to justify Sterling being killed.

East Baton Rouge Parish District Attorney Hillar Moore said Wednesday that Officers Blane Salamoni, a four-year BRPD veteran, and Howie Lake II, three-year veteran, told investigators that the shooting that killed Sterling was justified.

Could we imagine the police saying otherwise?

Of course the involved officers will defend a decision to shoot. The only open question is what the rest of us will say. Will Sterling's death change the hearts of those who've shrugged at the steady report of police guns? Will they finally acknowledge that the phrase "Black Lives Matter" arises from a place of anguish and sorrow?

Four years ago, President Barack Obama responded to Trayvon Martin's death like so many black Americans respond to such tragedies. We see ourselves and our relatives in the photos of the victims. "If I had a son, he'd look like Trayvon," Obama said.

When I look at Sterling's photos, I see my cousin Kevin, who died after years of health problems. Husky build. Gold tooth. Fade haircut. The recurring joke at his funeral was that he'd sold everybody in the family at least one CD. And not because we liked the music. We bought something to help him out.

You see, some of us have done more than nod at hustle man. Some of us have hugged him as family.

WHY NOT TRY TENDERNESS INSTEAD OF CORPORAL PUNISHMENT?

APRIL 9, 2017

At the Whitney Plantation in St. John the Baptist Parish, the Allées Gwendolyn Midlo Hall includes the names of 107,000 enslaved Africans brought to or born inside Louisiana. Interspersed between those names are first-hand accounts of what slavery was like according to those who experienced it.

"Sometimes I cried after I went to bed because of these whippin's," Hunlon Love reports. "Of course, it was necessary sometimes, but these overseers—grue-some men from the north—was brutal."

"Of course, it was necessary sometimes."

If you want proof that today's black people talk about whuppins the same way slaves talked about whippings, well, there it is engraved in stone.

I showed Stacey Patton the Hunlon Love quote Wednesday evening, and she wearily shook her head. It's a two-sentence distillation of her new book, "Spare the Kids: Why Whupping Children Won't Save Black

America," which argues that black people who praise the whuppings they got are unwittingly cosigning a brutal white supremacist practice.

"I hear that echo centuries later," Patton said of the Whitney Plantation quote: "I needed this. I'm the man I am today because somebody whupped me. It's so ingrained in our culture." Black parents, Patton said, "can't get over their fear that their child might not turn out fine" if they aren't physically overwhelmed when they are small.

"If getting whupped was a prerequisite for success," Patton said later to an audience at St. Peter Claver School, "then black people should be ruling the world right now."

Black people aren't the only folks in America who physically discipline their children, not by a long shot. According to Patton's book, "Between 70 and 80 percent of all Americans hit their children... Still, this book is solely focused on corporal punishment within the black community. It is an effort to understand how whupping children became so deeply embedded in our culture as good parenting." Research indicates, she says, that "black families report using physical punishment 10 percent more than parents from other communities."

One can grow up believing that whupping is just what all black people do and what all black people have always done. That was my belief. Then, almost 20 years ago, I read The Washington Post article "A good whuppin'?" that quoted a Howard University professor who said Africans didn't punish their children the way African-Americans punish theirs.

More recently I learned that my grandfather, born in rural Mississippi in 1910, never hit his children. According to my aunt, he kept them in line without ever raising his voice. That's not to say that my mother and her siblings were never whupped, and it's certainly not to say that they were anti-whupping. It is to note that there have always been people—even black people, even country black people—who've kept their hands to themselves.

Patton acknowledges that as big and diverse as Africa is that there's no "generalized, pancontinental statement" to be made about long-ago parenting practices. Even so, Murray Last, an emeritus professor at University College London and an expert on pre-colonial West African society, tells Patton for her book: "One can be sure that aggressive punishment against children in West Africa was unthinkable. To beat children was considered absurd. You might want to beat an adult for some infraction, but beating a child diminished you because an adult is older and more powerful."

Patton asked her St. Peter Claver audience to consider the names that West Africans gave their children. Babatunde means Father Has Returned; Yetunde, Mother Has Returned. Who would strike the embodiment of a beloved ancestor?

In Wednesday's column about Louisiana's death penalty, I said it's obviously not a deterrent if we have the nation's highest homicide rate. A reader responded, "How do we know there wouldn't have been more killings without it?" That, in a nutshell, is the typical black person's defense of whuppings. Whuppings, they say, keep children in line at school. Whuppings keep them from eventually going to prison. Point out the jaw-dropping number of suspensions and expulsions or the equally sickening numbers of black men and women in prison, and they say that there'd be even more without all those whuppings.

There are many people—sadly, many black people—who believe that black people and black children are fundamentally different than people of other races. This belief leads them to the conclusion that you have to have a stronger hand with black children, with black people. They don't believe that tenderness works or can work with black children. They believe that we need the whip, that we won't do right otherwise.

Last week a black woman in New Orleans uploaded to Facebook a selfie of her holding her 2-day-old son on her chest. The first two comments congratulated her. The third comment warned, "Don't spoil him."

Don't spoil him? If he can't get affection in the first 48 hours of his life, then when can he get it? If his mother can't be tender with him, then who will?

BY APOLOGIZING FOR SELLING SLAVES, GEORGETOWN HONORS THEIR DESCENDANTS

APRIL 23, 2017

> "And what shall we do, we who did not die? What shall we do now? How shall we grieve, and cry out loud, and face down despair? Is there an honorable non-violent means towards mourning and remembering who and what we loved?"
>   – June Jordan, "Some of Us Did Not Die"

*   *   *

After the news got out that Georgetown University sold off 272 human beings in 1838 to wiggle itself out of debt, and after Georgetown students staged a 2015 sit-in demanding the university change the names of buildings honoring those involved in that sale, a Georgetown official reportedly gave an implausible answer when asked about the fates of those sold.

According to multiple news reports, that unnamed university official told an alumnus inquiring about the university's shameful past that every one of the 272 "quickly succumbed to fever in the malodorous swamp world of Louisiana."

Wouldn't that have been convenient for Georgetown and the Jesuits who founded the university? If all those who were sold had died quickly, then Georgetown could never be confronted with living proof of its sin.

But according to GU272.net, a website for the descendants of those people sold by Georgetown into Louisiana, "what started in 1838 as 272 unshakable enslaved people is now more than 10,000 steadfast and determined descendants worldwide. Our ancestors did not perish in Louisiana! They flourished!"

I would have chosen a different verb—something closer to "survived" or "endured" or "lasted"—because to say they flourished implies a nurturing environment, and slave-holding Louisiana was anything but nurturing for those who were enslaved. But the point of GU272's declaration is that some of us did not die, even when we were consigned to the hellscape of a Louisiana plantation.

Cheryllyn Branche, a New Orleanian who is one of those descendants, said by phone Thursday that since the website went live in January, GU272 has found more than 800 descendants of that sale. Branche spoke to me from Washington where, earlier in the week, Georgetown renamed buildings that had honored Thomas F. Mulledy and William McSherry, past presidents of the university who participated in the sale and took in the filthy lucre.

The buildings are now named for Isaac Hawkins, whose name is listed first among the 272 humans who were sold, and for Anne Marie Becraft, a free person of color who opened a school for black girls in 1820 and later became one the country's first black nuns.

Georgetown also hosted a Liturgy of Remembrance, Contrition and Hope, attended by more than 100 descendants of the 272. At that ceremony, the Rev. Tim Kesicki, S.J., president of the Jesuit Conference of Canada and the United States, said, "Today the Society of Jesus, who helped to establish Georgetown University and whose leaders enslaved and mercilessly sold your ancestors, stands before you to say that we have greatly sinned. We pray with you today because we have greatly sinned and because we are profoundly sorry."

At the renaming ceremony, Karran Harper Royal, another New Orleanian who can trace her family's history back to the Georgetown 272, gave credit to those students who protested seeing the names of slave owners and peddlers on their buildings. "The actions of Georgetown students have placed all of us on a journey together toward honoring our enslaved ancestors by working toward healing and reconciliation," said Harper Royal, GU272's executive director. "This could have happened at any time in the history of Georgetown University, but it has happened now at a time when youth across this country are standing up to the injustices that they are witnessing in their communities and on their campuses."

Branche, 64, said all the events of the week—the liturgy, the renaming ceremony and tours that help them retrace some of their ancestors' steps—had left her feeling overwhelmed. "I was not prepared for the gravity of what I'm experiencing." She called it "difficult to digest and consume emotionally."

It was only May 2016 that Richard Cellini, the alum who says Georgetown told him that all 272 of the people they sold had died, called Branche to inform her how her people got to Louisiana. Hillary and Henny, her maternal grandmother's grandparents, and Basil, her grandmother's father, were loaded onto a ship and sold to a plantation in Ascension Parish. Who bought them? Henry Johnson, governor of Louisiana between 1824 and 1828.

The Jesuits' apology for their sin and Georgetown's decision to change the names of those buildings with relatively little defensiveness strikes me as the right thing to do. But Branche said that even now, there are people whose way of talking about slavery mitigates its evil.

As some of last week's tour guides explained, the Jesuits needed a cheap source of labor. So they had to own slaves. Branche couldn't believe that they would say the Jesuits "had to" own people even to those people's descendants.

But the self-described "strong Catholic" credits Georgetown and the Jesuits for such a public and meaningful apology. "They didn't just write it," Branche said. "They made sure it was televised."

WE CAN DISAGREE PASSIONATELY...BUT NOT VIOLENTLY

JUNE 16, 2017

During a recent walk amid lunch hour in downtown New Orleans, I turned off Canal Street and onto St. Charles Avenue. At that intersection I saw two women who worship as Jehovah's Witnesses. They were dressed conservatively, as most women associated with that denomination do, and they were standing next to a display printed with the question, "What does the Bible really teach?" A few steps past them stood a young woman with short-cropped, fluorescent hair. She wore a Planned Parenthood T-shirt and, as best I could tell, was seeking pedestrians' signatures on a petition to show support for that organization. I was thankful at that moment that I lived in America, a place where people with opposite political views could stand so close to one another without any noticeable friction.

Tuesday night, at my Baptist church in New Orleans, I was teaching two junior-high-school-age boys the story in 1 Samuel about the aftermath of David killing Goliath. King Saul decides to kill David after he hears women singing that Saul had killed thousands but David tens of thousands. The boys were confused, and I realized that much of their confusion owed to their being raised in a country that's so politically stable.

With the obvious exception of the Civil War, I told them, we haven't had a violent power struggle in the United States. But there are many places in our world where such violent political upheaval seems to always be a possibility, where people in power are constantly in fear of being overthrown.

The morning after that lesson, a 66-year-old Illinois man opened fire on a group of Republicans in Congress practicing on the diamond for their annual baseball game against the Democrats in Congress.

That gunman wounded Rep. Steve Scalise, the House majority whip from Jefferson who also represents my neighborhood in New Orleans. Scalise, who was shot in the hip, had surgery immediately after and was listed in critical condition. Three other people were injured: a congressional aide, a lobbyist and a Capitol police officer. The Capitol Police were at the baseball practice because of Scalise's leadership position in the House. Officers returned fire and killed the gunman.

Scalise's staunch conservatism is well known. So, too, is his affability and his remarkable ability to nurture meaningful friendships with people who disagree with his politics. His bromance with Rep. Cedric Richmond, now the leader of the Congressional Black Caucus, gets the most attention. But that's not the only example of his relationships with his political adversaries. State Sen. Karen Carter Peterson, chair of the Louisiana Democratic Party, issued a statement Wednesday morning. "I am deeply saddened and troubled that anyone would inflict terror on public servants," she wrote. "Steve Scalise is my friend and former state legislative colleague."

She also wrote, "I know personally that Steve and I share a core philosophy of standing up and fighting hard for what you believe in. He's strong and I look forward to his full recovery."

Looney Tunes had a series of cartoons in the 1950s and '60s featuring Sam Sheepdog and Ralph Wolf. They walk to work together as buddies with their arms draped over one another's shoulders. After they clock out from their jobs, they walk away the same way. But when they're actually at work and Ralph's trying to steal the sheep that Sam's protecting, they try to clobber the hell out of one another.

That analogy explains Scalise's relationship to Democrats and the Democrats' relationship to Scalise: We don't have to hate one another, but when we're in the arena, we're going to try to destroy you. And we can slap each other's backs and joke around later.

You can count me among those who disagree with Scalise on just about everything. Still, he's my representative in Congress, and it infuriates me that somebody shot him.

If there's enough room on a single city block for people with disparate political views, then there's certainly enough room in our country.

Surely we can passionately disagree with our political adversaries without seeking their annihilation.

CHARLOTTESVILLE SHOWS THE DANGERS OF CONFEDERATE STATUES

AUGUST 16, 2017

Let us not forget that the white nationalists who mobilized in Charlottesville over the weekend mobilized in defense of a statue of Robert E. Lee that officials in that city want to remove from a public park. A young woman is dead because somebody who rallied to defend the graven image of a defeated general ran over her with a car. Nineteen others were injured for the same abominable reason.

There should be no more debating about whether these monuments that blight the South are actually "white supremacist monuments." Their defenders have loudly objected to that characterization. But it should be plain now to them and to everybody else that white supremacist monuments are what they were meant to be. It's what they are, and it's why they must be removed.

All those who spoke up to defend Confederate monuments in New Orleans should be ashamed of themselves now. Charlottesville illustrates for them the side that they picked. The side of racism. The side of white nationalism. The side of violence. The side of murder.

And, to be sure, it was clear all the time that those statues represented that side—no matter how many so-called respectable people told us otherwise.

Over and over black people said, "These things are an offense. They cause us great pain. They were meant to terrorize us, to keep us in our place, to remind us of who's in charge, to mock what was then our forced subservience."

But, nah, supporters of the monuments to the White League and Jefferson Davis and P.G.T. Beauregard and Lee wanted to make it an academic exercise. They wanted to talk about slippery slopes and the erasure of history. They wanted to prattle on about how people fighting for the preservation of slavery were not racists but how some who fought for abolition were. They dared to compare the people wanting these obnoxious monuments removed to the Islamic State even as the monuments were being defended and valorized by America's own terrorist groups.

The Times-Picayune has photos from 1976 that show Ku Klux Klan members marching to the Liberty Monument when it was still at the foot of Canal Street. There's a photo from 1978 that shows Kalamu ya Salaam, spokesman for the Committee for Accountable Police, leading a counter rally after the Klan had gathered at that monument yet again. And there's an even more iconic photo of a New Orleans police officer holding the Rev. Avery Alexander in a near-chokehold as Alexander protests that monument. In the background, somebody's waving the Klan's favorite banner, the Confederate battle flag.

So, please, all you folks who thought it so important to fight to keep these monuments in place, don't pretend that you're just now learning who your allies were in that fight. It's never been unclear who your allies were: Nazis, Klansmen and white nationalists. And if it's true that the enemy of my enemy is my friend, then it is also true that the ally of my enemy is my enemy.

You had a chance to stand up for the oppressed, but you stood for and stood with the oppressors. Don't be surprised that 32-year-old Heather Heyer was killed as a result of a monument fight. Death goes hand in hand with white supremacy. All of us know that a belief in white supremacy led to the deaths of an untold number of black, brown and red people in this country. But the deaths of Andrew Goodman and Michael Schwerner in Mississippi and Viola Liuzzo, the Rev. James Reeb and Jonathan Daniels in Alabama remind us that white supremacists are willing to kill white people who oppose them.

The good news is that by rallying on behalf of a Confederate monument and killing somebody in the process, the hordes that descended on Charlottesville are actually hastening the removal of such monuments.

"I am taking action to relocate the Confederate statues," Mayor Jim Gray of Lexington, Kentucky tweeted Saturday.

Baltimore Mayor Catherine Pugh told The Baltimore Sun on Monday that she has talked to contractors about removal projects there. A commission recommended that Pugh's predecessor remove two of the city's four Confederate monuments, but Pugh said Monday, "We're looking at all four of them." That same day she said in a statement that she had consulted with Mayor Mitch Landrieu on how to proceed.

Also Monday, a group in Durham, North Carolina, took it upon themselves to pull down a Confederate

monument there. And, no, before you ask, their sabotage is not comparable to a man driving a car into a
crowd. I've previously argued that sabotage is not the
best way to respond to offensive monuments; still, I understand the righteous anger that erupted in Durham
on Monday.

A lie can't last forever. Confederate monuments are a
lie. They bestow honor on those who deserve none, and
they promote a distorted and perverted view of history.
For Heather Heyer's sake, for Avery Alexander's and for
so many others whose names we don't know, may each
of these monuments come down. And fast.

CANTRELL SHATTERS GLASS CEILING FOR TRANSPLANTS

NOVEMBER 22, 2017

There was a story I read recently—I wish I could remember where—about an adult who had moved to his small town to begin first grade. Well into his adulthood, that man was still being referred to as "the new guy." Though I can't remember where I read it, I was reading it in New Orleans, a city where people who are from here generally have more social status than those who are not.

In the race for the mayor of New Orleans, Desiree Charbonnet made sure to emphasize that she was born here. Her opponent, LaToya Cantrell, came here in 1990 to attend Xavier University. On social media, there were some supporters of Charbonnet who seemed to be at war with those who decided to move here. Charbonnet can't be blamed for what random people who were voting for her were saying or doing. However, at its core, that argument from her supporters was the same as the one Charbonnet was making: that when it comes to running the city, a native New Orleanian is necessarily better than a non-native New Orleanian.

But Saturday night, the new girl won. Cantrell, the transplant, ran away with victory, capturing three of every five votes cast in the race for mayor. We knew already that the election would be special. When Cantrell and Charbonnet got the most votes in the primary, we knew then that New Orleans would be led by a woman for the first time. But we didn't know if we'd continue the trend of going to the 7th Ward to find black mayors or if we'd elect somebody "Straight Outta Compton," as one of the nastier anti-Cantrell flyers described her.

Cantrell won the 7th Ward. In fact, with the exception of Lakeview, she won all over the city, taking 331 of the 351 precincts. Charbonnet tried to tackle Cantrell with allegations that she misused her city credit card, but Cantrell not only survived, she essentially walked into the end zone.

The irony is that for all Charbonnet's talk of being from here, voters seemed to have more faith in Cantrell's concern for the people. Maybe voters trusted her more because they remember how she got her hands dirty bringing Broadmoor back to life before she was an elected official. Or maybe they questioned Charbonnet's concern because she had District Attorney Leon Cannizzaro and Rep. Steve Scalise on her side. Both men are polarizing figures in New Orleans, and a black woman seeking their support is taking a huge risk for what's likely to be a low reward.

Beyond that, Charbonnet's decision to trumpet endorsements from Scalise and Rep. Maxine Waters may have made voters wonder if she had any fixed positions. Bridge-building is great, and we need more people who can talk to and work with people with whom they disagree, but shouldn't a black, native New Orleanian know that touting a Scalise endorsement during a mayoral election would turn people off like wieners in a gumbo?

In the weeks after Hurricane Katrina, demographer William Frey explained that New Orleans is one of the most rooted cities in the country. Rootedness is measured by the number of people in a city who were born in that city or nearby. New Orleanians tend to see rootedness as a positive. It confirms that people love this city so much that they rarely leave. But Frey pointed out that if a city has a sky-high percentage of people who are native born, then that means nobody's choosing to move to that city.

And shouldn't we want to be the kind of city to which people want to move?

That's not to dismiss the reality that New Orleans and its neighborhoods are changing in ways that scare many residents who've spent their whole lives here. Nor is it to deny that many (if not most) of the changes are related to the arrivals of people who are moving here from elsewhere. That said, it's hard to imagine a city that is simultaneously attractive to people who were born here and unattractive to those who were not.

Income inequality and wealth disparities help explain much of the tension between original New Orleanians and new New Orleanians. New Orleans is becoming more expensive, and people who move here from elsewhere seem to have more money. Cantrell will have many challenges during a mayoral term. One of her biggest challenges will be helping New Orleanians better afford the city they love. Are there economic development strategies that transform the lives of people who are already here? Are there ways to make housing more affordable? Voters are counting on her to address these problems.

We can be sure that the social status that derives from being born in New Orleans won't change with one person's election. But if Cantrell is successful, she will be helping put an end to the idea that those who choose New Orleans aren't qualified to serve New Orleans. New people can lead, too, especially when by "new" we mean a resident of 27 years.

THE COLUMN I WISH I COULD TAKE BACK

DECEMBER 13, 2017

Readers sometimes ask me if there's any column that I've written that I wish I could take back. My general answer is no. There may be issues on which my thinking has shifted some, but as long as my columns reflect the way that I was thinking at the time, I don't feel any need to be embarrassed by them.

There is one glaring exception, though. Ten years ago I wrote an especially mean column about Kathleen Babineaux Blanco. I attacked her for sport. I mocked and belittled her unnecessarily, and when I look back at what I wrote, I feel ashamed.

That old column is the first thing that popped into my mind when I heard that the former governor is ailing with metastatic cancer: that I owe her an apology, one that she can read while she is still with us. I owe it to her even though I pray she's forgotten the insult. So here it is:

Governor, I'm sorry for being mean just for the sake of being mean. Criticizing your policies and the execution of your policies was fair game. Going beyond that and mocking you personally, as I did in one column, was mean-spirited and cruel, and it belied my home training. You are a good and decent person, and you've exhibited that goodness and decency at every turn. Public service can't be easy, especially when some of us on press row are acting like asses.

Readers will understand, I hope, why I'm choosing not to repeat the insults I made 10 years ago. It would be counterproductive to republish them at a time when I'm apologizing for them. Also, with so many more people on social media now than then, there's the chance that more people could see it now. See it at the time when Blanco, who turns 75 this week, is most deserving of the public's love and support. As the former governor wrote in an open letter that was published by NOLA.com | The Times-Picayune over the weekend, "I would deeply appreciate, if you should see fit, that you offer prayers on behalf of myself, as well as all others fighting to survive life-threatening illnesses."

So I won't repeat the offense. Please take my word for it that I was out of line.

Before Hurricane Katrina, I wrote a column once a week. After Katrina, the frequency increased to three times a week. Two years after that, I was still experimenting with voice. I decided to channel a columnist whose writing I admired and practice the art of the insult.

In a strictly technical sense, I believe the column worked, but my motivations weren't right, and, thus, I was wrong. I wasn't trying to advance a cause. I wasn't championing a policy. I wasn't sticking up for somebody who needed advocacy. And because Blanco had decided against seeking a second term and because the election for her successor had already been held, I wasn't even sticking it to the powerful. I was just having some fun at her expense. It was gratuitous in every way.

In the 10 years since then, I have written passionate columns. I have written angry columns. I have written columns that I intended to be comical or mocking, but I don't think I've ever written another column that was just flat-out mean. And I shouldn't have written that one. She didn't deserve it.

None of this should be interpreted as an apology for columns critical of the Road Home debacle. She deserved all the criticism she got for that—especially given her choice to name it Governor Kathleen Babineaux Blanco's Road Home Program. Louisiana Republicans were initially angry at her for putting her name in front of that program the way that Hollywood megastars put their names above the title of a blockbuster movie. Then, as the program inspired anger across the state, those same Republican critics found themselves glad that everybody saw her name on it. When Blanco phoned me to complain about my criticism of her and her program, I told her that maybe it had been a bad idea for her to put her name on it. She said she hadn't. I said, "You never called it the Kathleen Babineaux Blanco Road Home Program?!" loud enough for my colleagues in the office to stare in disbelief.

I still chuckle at her response: "I'll have to check."

Despite that momentary denial of the obvious, that reluctance to admit that she had invited the Road Home failures on herself, I still believe that Blanco is a fundamentally honest person who happened to be governor at one of the most difficult times in Louisiana history. If we'd had the kind of federal response the crisis required, then there wouldn't have been so much anger directed at her. We shouldn't lose sight of how humongous the job was and how much criticism—justified or otherwise—was directed at her.

In the letter announcing the gravity of her medical predicament, Blanco writes: "It has been an honor and blessing to have been chosen, like Esther, to lead our people at such a time as this. Again, please add me to your prayer list. I hope I can survive and thrive as you have done."

I hope she survives and thrives, too. And I hope that the rest of her days—however many there are—are filled with people expressing their appreciation and thanks.

MITCH LANDRIEU'S NEW BOOK:
A self-portrait of a mayor who is dogged and a bit naïve

MARCH 21, 2018

It is nearly impossible for a white person to arrive at an epiphany about America's history of racial oppression that will double as an epiphany to the average black person. New Orleans Mayor Mitch Landrieu was made to see and care about the Confederate monuments littering his city by black people who had been aggravated by them for as long as they could remember and by black people who hated explaining to their children why they existed.

Black people made the white mayor understand, and then he asked other white people to see the offense as he led his government's effort to take the monuments down.

Landrieu's book, "In the Shadow of Statues: A White Southerner Confronts History," is the outgoing mayor's latest attempt to convince white people in the South that Civil War mythologies they may have swallowed whole are mythologies that most black people have always rejected as poison.

Landrieu said in June 2015 that his desire to remove monuments to Robert E. Lee, the White League, P.G.T.

Beauregard and Jefferson Davis was inspired by a conversation with New Orleans-born trumpeter Wynton
Marsalis. In the book, he says Marsalis agreed to participate in the city's tricentennial activities but, in exchange, asked Landrieu to think about taking down
Lee.

Landrieu responds, "You lost me on that."

He quotes Marsalis saying, "I don't like the fact that
Lee Circle is named Lee Circle," and himself responding, "Why is that?"

This is a scene that we should all sit with and contem-
plate. Here you have a New Orleans-born white man in
his fifties asking a New Orleans-born black man who's
a year younger why the name Lee Circle bothers him.

In telling his life story, Landrieu makes it a point to
talk about the number of black friends he had. His father, Moon Landrieu, is best friends with Norman Francis, the longtime president of Xavier University, and
the Landrieu children grew up playing with the Francis children. Mayor Moon Landrieu hired black professionals to work at City Hall, which many white people,
his son writes, interpreted as the elder Landrieu turning the city "over to the blacks." Mitch Landrieu had
multiple black opponents when he ran for mayor in
2010 and 2014 and won the black vote convincingly.

And yet, the offensiveness of the Lee monument still
needed to be explained to him.

I asked the mayor Friday that if he didn't get it, how
can white people with limited experiences with black
people get it? He said he thought the public's increas-
ing support for marriage equality suggested that people can change but not before he labeled my question
"hopeless."

Perhaps it is. But it's hard feeling hopeful when Landrieu devotes half his book to laying out his and his family's legacy challenging racism and the other half explaining how he was blind to something most black people couldn't help seeing.

The Landrieus' legacy on race notwithstanding, Mitch Landrieu still possessed a naïveté that black readers may find curious.

In 2006, the first mayoral election after Hurricane Katrina, Landrieu lost to Ray Nagin after Nagin won black people who feared a loss of black political strength. "Ray Nagin beat me at his weakest moment!" Landrieu said Friday, explaining that he never intended to run for mayor. Addressing his loss to Nagin in his book, Landrieu writes, "I was hurt, mostly because this was one of the few times I realized people viewed me as white."

But he is white. How else could he be viewed?

It is inconceivable that a Southern black man of 45—the age Landrieu was when Nagin beat him—could have an experience that prompts him to the realization that people see him as black.

And that may be the book's saddest and most significant reminder: White people, even white people named Landrieu, can choose not to see or think about race. Black people can't.

At the height of the debate over monuments, an untold number of white people said something that betrayed their belief that because they hadn't given those monuments a passing thought that black people couldn't possibly have been angered by them. It is a hallmark of white privilege to believe that what white people don't know, don't feel or don't think about isn't known, felt or thought about by anybody.

Landrieu had the option to dismiss black people's simmering anger and disgust at the monuments, but he decided to take their feelings seriously. He underestimated the backlash that would occur. He underestimated the amount of time and the amount of money it would take to take them down, but he saw that they came down.

It cost him many white people's support. But, he said Friday, "I feel stronger about it today" than he felt during the long process of removal.

He can't win a statewide election anymore, but he says he gave up his dream of being governor once he became mayor. "I governed like it was the end of the road," he said. "This is it." Then he added, "which is fine."

FROM "JENA 6" DEFENDANT TO AGITATOR FOR JUSTICE
With law degree in hand, Theo Shaw says he has a responsibility to fulfill

JUNE 6, 2018

If we've learned nothing else in this current age, it's that a man who appears to be one thing in public can be something else in private. The person who says and does all the right things when he's aware of an audience can be a monster in his private, interpersonal interactions. There are limits to what we can know about another. People have the capacity for good and bad, greatness and depravity, and they can disappoint us just as much as they can inspire.

But even during this era, when the safe bet is on assuming the worst, it is impossible to think that Theo Shaw has ever been fundamentally different from the gentle spirit who led his law school class into an auditorium at the University of Washington Sunday night and gave his class a valediction to do justice and agitate on behalf of the poor.

People can change. People can be rehabilitated. But if there's anybody whose good character seems locked in and immutable, if there's anyone whose character should make us doubt a past allegation against him, it's Shaw.

One simply can't conceive of him setting upon a high school classmate with an intent to kill.

But in December 2006, in a case that drew worldwide attention and led to thousands of protesters marching in Jena, Theodore Rosevelt Shaw, then 17, was one of six black teenagers from Jena High School accused of attempted murder in an attack on a white student at the school.

The victim was treated in an emergency room, so somebody obviously attacked him. But Shaw says he didn't, and it takes more cynicism than I possess to believe he's lying.

Despite his claims of innocence, to make the case go away, he eventually pleaded no contest to simple battery, a misdemeanor. If a jury had found him guilty of the original attempted murder charge, Shaw could have been imprisoned well into his 60s.

But there he was Sunday night, at age 29, standing out in a room of legal scholars. The Class of 2018 at the UW School of Law chose him to speak for them and to them.

Even the law professor who called him forward to receive his degree was effusive with praise. He introduced Shaw as "my beyond student" and said, "I learned so much from him. I hope he learned something from me."

Shaw's story is a cautionary tale, but not the typical cautionary tale one tells to scare a misbehaving child into straightening up. It's a cautionary tale that law enforcement officers in this incarceration-happy state of ours need to digest. How many other Theo Shaws has our criminal justice system chewed up and destroyed?

How much talent is drying up in the sun on Angola plantation?

Emily Maw, the senior counsel for Innocence Project New Orleans, was in Seattle Sunday night to see Shaw lead his law school classmates into the auditorium.

"Of course he's exceptional," she said Monday, but focusing on his exceptionality "misses the point." After his time in jail, she said, he had a network of people who cared for him and advocated for him, who provided mentoring and guidance. "It shows what kids that we would otherwise throw away can do," Maw said.

Maybe others wouldn't be law-school standouts, she said, but they could still achieve. "That's the moral of the story."

Maw was in Seattle with her husband, Rob McDuff, the attorney who negotiated Shaw's plea deal and helped him get his life back on track.

"It was quite a sight," McDuff said, "to see this young man who Louisiana incarcerated on unreasonably high bail, who was on the railroad to the penitentiary, leading his class, leading the procession, giving the speech to the law school graduation. I don't know that that's ever happened!"

*   *   *

Shaw interrupted his bar studies Friday to talk to me about law school and the speech he was scheduled to give two days later. I reminded him that in 2014 he told me that he had no direction when he was a high school senior, that he had no plans after high school and that he believes he was ranked dead last in his class.

"Were you a different person then?" I asked him. "Was there a transformation so profound that Theo Shaw became a different person than he was in high school, or were you just this diamond in the rough kind of thing where all the traits you have now were actually there, but you just weren't clicking yet? How do you see it?"

He said he was always likable and that it wasn't his personality that changed but his focus.

"I think it was Frederick Douglass who said, 'Some people know the value of education by having it. I know its value by not having it,'" Shaw said.

While in jail, he borrowed a law book from another inmate and began writing motions to get the judge to lower his bail. He said in an interview before law school that he felt a rush of power when he realized that even as a poor, uneducated, incarcerated teenager, he could write something that compelled a judge to respond—if only to say no.

In Friday's interview, he told me that having his jailhouse motions denied taught him, "Oh, I have to just talk the way you want me to talk, and maybe they'll come give me some attention."

McDuff met Shaw when he was out of jail but still had charges hanging over his head. "First thing he said to me when I met with him was, 'I want to get back into school.' Didn't talk about his case. Said, 'I want to get back in school.' I went to talk to the guidance counselor, principal. They all loved Theo. We worked it out, got him back in school. It's amazing how he turned that terrible experience into a true quest."

"There was a transformation in terms of his ambition," McDuff said, "but I think the underlying qualities that caused him to pursue that ambition" haven't changed.

"During his case, he was calm, collected, he took every-thing in stride, he kept a positive view, he had perspec-tive, he looked at the big picture. It was really amazing." The day Shaw ended his case by pleading to a misde-meanor, the victim in the Jena High attack was sitting in the front row of the courtroom, McDuff remembers. "Theo went over and shook his hand and wished him the best for the future. His goodness was always there."

*   *   *

On Friday afternoon, Shaw was still figuring out what he was going to say for Sunday night's speech. "I don't know," he said when I asked what he had planned. "I do mock trials in law school, and I usually have bullet points of what to talk about. I think when I stand up I'll sort of let my convictions or heart just move me where I feel like I should be going."

When he stood at the lectern Sunday, he didn't bring bullet points. He extemporized. He spoke of the intern-ship Maw made possible at IPNO and how that job al-lowed him to meet inmates at Angola who are all free now thanks to that organization's advocacy.

"I talk about those men's experience because after to-night, after the celebration, even after we pass the bar, I believe as future lawyers, we have a responsibility," he said. "We may not be guilty or have had anything to do with the injustices that other people experienced in the criminal justice system. But we have a responsibility: a responsibility to the poor, to the condemned, to those who may not be popular in the eyes of the majority."

Despite his own remarkable story as one of the Jena 6, he didn't mention any part of it in his speech. He didn't even mention that years after he failed to persuade a judge in his home parish to lower his bail, he persuaded the highest-ranking judge in the state to hire him for a clerkship.

"This is an inspiring young man who's overcome significant obstacles," Louisiana Chief Justice Bernette Johnson said on the phone Tuesday. "Instead of being discouraged, what he's done is work harder."

Johnson praised Shaw's "great focus" and his "great analytical skills" and called him "the full package. I'm looking at potential, people who want to make a difference. I want a legacy of law clerks who want to make a difference."

In March 2017, almost two years after my column announcing Shaw's acceptance to law school, it had a second life of Internet virality. People were sharing it on Twitter and Facebook like it had just happened when, by that time, it was old news. People shared it with Shaw, too. As if he didn't know.

Why does he think his story has resonated so powerfully with so many people?

"It's not often you turn on the TV and see the media talking favorably about a young black man. Most of the time you turn on the TV, it's about crime and all this bad stuff," he said. "I think for our community that any time there is sort of something to change that narrative about us, people like to put that out there."

Black people crave reminders "that who they say we are we're not. Actually, this is who we are. And at that point, it's not even just about me. It's about us. This is us. Yes, he went to law school and did great things, but this is about us as a people. This is who we are."

Shaw's father, who worked at an apparel manufacturing plant in Jena, passed away during his son's second year in law school. Not that there can ever be a substitute for one's own father, but it was clear from a conversation with Wayne Brumfield, a former vice president at the University of Louisiana Monroe, that he's a quasi-father in Shaw's life. It was Brumfield who began mentoring Shaw when he transferred from Louisiana Delta Community College.

He knew the story of what happened in Jena but finds the idea of Shaw's involvement as preposterous as I do.

"It's hard to imagine Theo being a violent person," he said and described the charges against him as "trumped up."

Like the law professor who called Shaw to the stage to receive his degree, Brumfield said, "I learned a lot from him, believe it or not: When things don't seem to go the way they should, just keep pushing forward."

But on Sunday night in Seattle, it was Brumfield who let Shaw know that he could stop pushing—if only for a minute. Two of Shaw's cousins traveled from Jena to see him graduate. His brother drove over from another part of Washington.

Shaw told them after the commencement that he needed to return home to resume studying for the bar. Brumfield was still laughing Monday at the absurdity of that.

"Take a little break, man," he said he told him. "You got your brother and your cousins. Take a little break. You good."

WHY DOESN'T LOUISIANA HAVE A CIVIL RIGHTS MUSEUM?

DECEMBER 5, 2018

Deep inside the Mississippi Civil Rights Museum in Jackson, a visitor turns a corner and is confronted with a larger-than-life-size photo of two black civil rights activists arriving at a Jackson bus terminal where they know they will be arrested for entering a whites-only waiting room.

The two self-sacrificing activists—Doris Jean Castle and Jerome Smith—are New Orleanians, and the photo of them looks like it's been snipped out of a black-and-white action movie. Smith is in stride and holds a suitcase with both hands at waist level; Castle, a purse dangling from her left wrist, holds a Birmingham newspaper in the same hand. "Riders vow..." is the only part of the front-page headline we can see. But the resolute look on their faces finishes the thought. It is obvious they vow to keep going.

Even if it means being thrown into a Mississippi jail cell.

A New Orleanian standing in that museum three hours north feels a twin rush of pride and embarrassment. The pride comes from the realization that the civil rights contributions of New Orleanians are recognized outside New Orleans. But that pride is quickly supplanted by embarrassment that those civil rights contributions are not properly recognized within this state.

Alabama has the Civil Rights Institute in Birmingham. Georgia has long had the King Center for Nonviolent Social Change in Atlanta, the city where Martin Luther King Jr. was born. More recently, Atlanta became home to the National Center for Civil and Human Rights. Tennessee has the National Civil Rights Museum; it's at the site of Memphis' Lorraine Motel, where King was assassinated. And then in December 2017, just in time for a celebration of the state's bicentennial, Mississippi opened the doors of the Mississippi Civil Rights Museum.

Louisiana, shamefully, has nothing.

Louisiana has nothing even though it was New Orleans civil rights activity that led to the 1896 Plessy v. Ferguson ruling, one of the most wrongheaded and consequential Supreme Court decisions in American history.

Louisiana has nothing even though a 1953 bus boycott the Rev. T.J. Jemison led in Baton Rouge inspired a larger, world-changing bus boycott that kicked off in Montgomery, Alabama, two years later.

Louisiana has nothing even though Jemison and King, the leader of the Montgomery boycott, were among those who met at Central City's New Zion Baptist Church to help start a new organization called the Southern Christian Leadership Conference.

Louisiana has nothing even though the first group of Freedom Riders leaving Washington set New Orleans as their destination; even though the photo of Ruby Bridges walking solo into William Frantz Elementary School is one of the most iconic images of the era; even though the young people who sat in at the McCrory's lunch counter in New Orleans in 1963 successfully challenged their arrests in a Supreme Court case called Lombard v. Louisiana.

That ruling put an end to many segregationist laws across the country. And yet, there's no museum here that recognizes the heroism and accomplishments of Rudy Lombard, Lanny Goldfinch, Cecil Carter Jr. and Oretha Castle, the older sister of the woman who's featured in the aforementioned photo in the museum in Mississippi.

Adding to Louisiana's shame is this bit of history: Diana Bajoie, a Louisiana state senator who represented New Orleans, authored a bill that establishes the Louisiana Civil Rights Museum and mandates that it be built in New Orleans. The bill passed the state legislature—in 1999.

Today, nearly two decades later, New Orleanians still have to leave the state to find a museum that tells the story of the civil rights movement.

Attorney Ernest Jones, an advisory board member for the Louisiana Civil Rights Museum, says he hasn't yet been able to bring himself to visit the new civil rights museum in Jackson.

It breaks his heart, he said, that Mississippi, which started planning a museum long after Louisiana did, has opened the doors to its museum, and Louisiana hasn't even gotten as far as selecting a location.

Jones believes that Louisiana's role in this country's civil rights movement hasn't been adequately appreciated. "We had folks here in this town doing stuff that folks don't know anything about," he said.

A major goal of a museum would be to help young people see themselves as capable of producing change, he said.

"I think what our young folks need is an idea, a role model," Jones said. He wants them to see and learn about a particular civil rights activist's story and walk away thinking of him or her as "a person just like me."

Why doesn't Louisiana have a civil rights museum 19 years after Gov. Mike Foster signed Bajoie's bill? The most direct answer appears to be that no one with sufficient clout has made the project a priority.

"I think if I'd stayed a little longer, I could've got it done," Bajoie said. But, "I got term limited." She senses a lack of passion from her successors. "You got to make the votes," she said. "If you don't have that passion, it's kind of hard to get people to do things."

What little money there is for the project, Jones said, can't be used until the museum is shovel ready. It's unlikely that day will come until somebody with power—say, the mayor of New Orleans or the governor or lieutenant governor of Louisiana—forces a decision about the museum's location.

As is typical for the state's appointed boards and commissions, the Civil Rights Museum Advisory Board does not have a budget, and its members do not receive a salary, a per diem or reimbursements if and when they travel. That wouldn't mean much if everybody on the board was from New Orleans. But it's meant to be a state civil rights museum; by law, there must be at least one member of the board from each congressional district.

The governor, lieutenant governor and chancellor of Southern University in Baton Rouge are also authorized to appoint people to the board. But if they pick people from outside New Orleans, some portion of the board will have to travel and pay for those travel costs out of pocket.

"We don't have any staff," Jones said, and "no office." Even sending out notices of public meetings is a challenge, he said.

In addition to establishing the advisory board, the 1999 legislation mandates that the museum "be operated, managed, and funded by the office of the state museum of the Department of Culture, Recreation and Tourism"—that is, by the lieutenant governor's office.

Bill Sherman, communications director for Lt. Gov. Billy Nungesser, said in response to an inquiry from NOLA.com | The Times-Picayune: "The Lt. Gov. has not had any contact with N.O. officials regarding a location of a CR museum. However, there have been some preliminary in-house discussions about possibly locating a room(s) in an existing museum that could host a CR exhibit. At this time, the Louisiana State Museum is struggling to keep up with repairs and maintenance at existing museums with their limited budget."

A room inside a larger museum is not what the 1999 legislation establishes. Neither is Louisiana's African American Heritage Trail, which Mitch Landrieu created when he was lieutenant governor.

Calling the museum project "an unfunded mandate," Shauna Sanford, communications director for Gov. John Bel Edwards, blamed the "$2 billion budget deficit" Edwards faced when he was inaugurated.

"While we are making progress, funding for existing expenses is limited," Sanford said, "which does not leave room for funding operating expenses on new projects at this time."

Mississippi found money.

The Mississippi Legislature in 2011 approved $40 million in bonds with the caveat that half of that money be reimbursed with private donations.

Mississippi actually built two museums with a single entrance—one that tells the entire history of the state and the other that focuses on the struggle for civil rights. An October 2017 column in The Clarion-Ledger suggests that the two-museum idea made the civil rights museum more palatable. However, it's doubtful that even that idea would have gotten off the ground if not for then-Gov. Haley Barbour's State of the State address in 2011.

Barbour, who was then considering running for president in 2012, said at that time: "The civil rights struggle is an important part of our history, and millions of people are interested in learning more about it. People from around the world would flock to see the museum and learn about the movement."

And they have. Mississippi had projected that they'd get 180,000 visitors to their two museums in the first year. As of late October, they'd gotten 233,956.

The June 2012 Louisiana Civil Rights Museum Planning Study compares Louisiana's proposed civil rights museum with others around the country. A civil rights museum in New Orleans, the study concludes, should expect to do better than the one in Greensboro, North Carolina because New Orleans is bigger and a more popular tourist destination. But it shouldn't expect to do as well as the museum in Memphis, which is something like a shrine to Martin Luther King Jr.

"We are in an era when African American-related history and culture is becoming more prominent in museums and venues around the country, indicating a growing interest," the report says.

In the six years since that planning report was published, the National Center for Civil and Human Rights in Atlanta and the Mississippi Civil Rights Museum have opened. So, too, has the National Memorial for Peace and Justice in Montgomery, Alabama, a six-acre site dedicated to the more than 4,400 black people lynched in America between 1877 and 1950.

"I know I'm paranoid," Ernest Jones said when we met to discuss the stalled progress of a Louisiana civil rights museum, "but I have an abiding sense that the enemies of my people don't want this to exist."

Site selection has proved to be especially difficult. Initially, the old Myrtle Banks Elementary School Building on Oretha Castle Haley Boulevard was the museum board's top choice for the museum. Turry Flucker, a branch director for the state Department of Culture, Recreation and Tourism, said in 2004, "I think the site is fantastic. It's accessible to the public and in a neighborhood where much of the modern civil rights movement occurred."

A feasibility study would have to be done, Flucker added, and that could take two years, maybe more. Then came Hurricane Katrina. And three years after that, a fire.

In 2011, Lourdes Moran, then the president of the Orleans Parish School Board, said the board would be auctioning off decrepit buildings. Alembic Community Development purchased the old school building for

$660,000 and currently uses it to house Dryades Public Market.

In 2013, the civil rights museum board bid $8.2 million for the Arts Council of New Orleans' ArtWorks building on the corner of Howard Avenue and Carondelet Street. Though the board's bid was reportedly $2 million more than The New Orleans Culinary & Hospitality Institute, which was awarded the building, guild board chairman Bill Hines told The Lens that the council was not obligated to choose the highest bidder and that the civil rights museum board's proposed financing was less secure than NOCHI's.

Before Mitch Landrieu left office as mayor, Jones said, the board proposed housing the museum in the four cottages in Armstrong Park that the National Park Service has since relinquished to the city. The idea of using the Municipal Auditorium for that purpose has also been floated.

Jones, who was appointed to the museum board by Landrieu when he was mayor, said that the board has not yet had any conversations with Mayor LaToya Cantrell about the museum or where it might go.

"Mayor Cantrell is open to engagement on this issue, and welcomes input regarding the site location and any other considerations," said City Communications Director Michael Tidwell. "While this project specifically has not been on our front burner, issues of equity, social justice and taking an honest look at our history are major priorities for the mayor."

Jones said the board's last meeting with a quorum was in July. What was on the agenda?

"How can we get a location?" Jones said. "And how can we get some money?"

What about getting a champion, somebody with power who can get things rolling?

Jones laughed. "That should be on the agenda," he said.

The exhibit at the Mississippi Civil Rights Museum that features Smith and Castle is not really about the two of them, per se. Yes, it shows their likenesses, but it's actually an exhibit about a favorite trick of segregationists: labeling all civil rights activists communists.

At the bottom corner of the exhibit, there's the image of an open file folder. It's labeled "Freedom Riders," and inside there's an official-looking report and a newspaper headline: "RIDERS TIED TO 'COMMIES.'" The subhead reads: "Patrol Officials Claim Communists in State."

When Smith was shown a cellphone photo of the exhibit in Jackson, he lit up.

"That's Doris!" he said, remembering his fellow activist who died 20 years ago.

Smith talked about how brave the women in the movement were, how their bravery so often inspired his own. He talked about how upset he'd been during that particular demonstration. Why did he have to put on a suit and tie, he was wondering, just to get arrested?

There was no discussion about the accusation that they were communists. Smith referred to a conversation he'd had with King and how impressed King had been with Smith's ability to express theological truths in ways that were understandable to the people they were attempting to mobilize.

Then he explained the method he used to connect with older folks who may have been suspicious of young people and their activism.

"Ma'am, I'm with the student movement," Smith said he'd tell the person answering the door, "and we're out here trying to advance the teachings of the Sermon on the Mount." How could church-going elders say no to that?

Every conversation with Smith is a history lesson, and he seems willing to share his experiences with anybody who asks him to share it. But he can't talk to everybody, and like everybody else's, his time on this planet is limited.

The legislature, in its wisdom, decided in 1999 that there needs to be a museum that holds Smith's stories and the stories of so many others in New Orleans and Louisiana who fought for the meek and who hungered and thirsted for righteousness.

In his most famous address, King imagines that "even the state of Mississippi, a state sweltering with the heat of injustice, sweltering with the heat of oppression, will be transformed into an oasis of freedom and justice."

The state hasn't come that far, but, in 2018, we can truthfully say that even Mississippi has celebrated and commemorated its civil rights heroes.

Louisiana has done nothing.

COLUMNISTS WORTHY OF THE TITLE CAN'T BE AFRAID OF UPSETTING SOMEONE

JULY 1, 2018

My first column for The Times-Picayune, published 20 years ago this June when I was still a reporter, began by explaining to readers what I am not. "I am not a nigger," it began. "I know this because one fall afternoon when I was 7 years old, my father told me I wasn't.

"It did not matter, he told me, how those two white boys up the road had just greeted me; that word did not describe who or what I was. He didn't use that famous 'sticks and stones' line; he knew the word could hurt. He just begged me to stop crying and told me repeatedly what a good person I was."

I have written thousands of columns since, but that one—a response to Merriam-Webster's decision to keep printing and defining the word "nigger" in its lexicon—was my first for The Times-Picayune. I believe that I accomplished in that inaugural opinion piece something that I try to accomplish with the columns I write 20 years later. I believe I managed to be unpredictable and thoughtful, open to other viewpoints without minimizing or subverting my own.

In that June 23, 1998, column, I described how the word had been used against the black people who raised me and me and the black people I was raised with. I described how we used the word to talk to and describe one another, sometimes with bitterness and disappointment, sometimes with humor and affection. I pushed back on the ridiculous and ahistorical notion that black people using the epithet had inspired white people to adopt it. I said I didn't care what Merriam-Webster printed. I better trusted my daddy to tell me who I am.

Wednesday morning, a local pastor introduced me to a book called "How to Preach a Dangerous Sermon" by Frank A. Thomas, a professor of homiletics and the director of the Academy of Preaching and Celebration at Christian Theological Seminary in Indianapolis. I told the pastor that the book might double as instruction on how to write a dangerous column

Indeed. "If at least some of my sermons are not dangerous," Thomas writes in his preface, "I lose a piece of my integrity." Similarly, there have been times when a colleague has predicted that a column about to be published will get me in trouble. I've laughed and said, "What good is a columnist who doesn't get in trouble?"

I grew up in the same town as anti-lynching crusader and journalist Ida B. Wells. So, I've never had the luxury of thinking of the best, most effective journalism as being anything less than dangerous.

I grew up near Memphis, Tennessee, where white people destroyed the Memphis Free Speech, the newspaper Wells co-owned, after she defended three black friends who were attacked for running a grocery that took customers away from white grocery stores; the grocers were taken to jail when they shot back at their attackers and subsequently dragged out of jail and lynched.

"The city of Memphis has demonstrated that neither character nor standing avails the Negro if he dares to protect himself against the white man or become his rival," Wells wrote. "There is nothing we can do about the lynching now, as we are outnumbered and without arms. The white mob could help itself to ammunition without pay, but the order is rigidly enforced against the selling of guns to Negroes. There is therefore only one thing left to do; save our money and leave a town which will neither protect our lives and property, nor give us a fair trial in the courts, but takes us out and murders us in cold blood when accused by white persons."

I don't suggest that I'm a Wells, that I will ever be a Wells or that 2018 is 1892. But I have always considered it a responsibility, a duty, to speak up for the people at risk of being crushed by the powerful. And I can't let the idea of powerful people getting upset be much of my concern.

To return to the preaching analogy, Thomas writes in his book, "Many clergypersons choose to be silent, realizing that 'politics' is polarizing, and the best thing is not to offend anyone by saying or doing anything that could remotely be conceived of as 'controversial.'"

And the comments sections are filled with people who accuse those who inveigh against injustice of being no different than the purveyors of injustice they're writing about.

This column was conceived before a gunman, who was still seething over a 2011 column, killed five peo-

ple and severely wounded others Thursday at the Capital Gazette newspaper in Annapolis, Maryland. But
Thursday's shooting makes plain that the danger we've
been talking about is not hyperbole—that it is real
danger. I don't want to elaborate about the times that I
have been threatened. Just know that there have been
threats, some less veiled than others. Just know that the
threats won't work.

Just like that first column began with a description of
what I'm not, let this one end in a similar fashion: I am
not afraid.

SAYING GOODBYE TO A PLACE THAT WILL ALWAYS BE HOME

JUNE 28, 2019

Weeks before I left for New Orleans to begin an internship at The Times-Picayune, I reached out to Greg Freeman, the metro columnist for the St. Louis Post-Dispatch. And he was gracious enough to have lunch with me, a senior from his alma mater, and listen to me fret about the future.

I'd probably be assigned to write crime stories, I said, but I didn't want to make black people look bad. What should I do?

Freeman, himself a black man, chuckled softly. Then he said, "You tell the truth."

Seven months later, on a warm December Saturday night at the Fischer housing complex, I found the mother of a man who'd just been shot, and then I found the mother of the teenager who'd pulled the trigger. After I interviewed them both, they hugged, and the mother of the gunman gave the other a kiss and apologized. "I'm sorry that happened. I didn't raise him like that."

"We're only mothers," her neighbor said. "It's not our fault."

And just like that I realized that telling the truth meant more than just reporting that one black person had shot another; it meant reporting the exchange between two women who refused to become enemies because their sons were fighting. So much reporting on troubled neighborhoods focuses on the trouble without even mentioning the neighbors. But if we're going to tell the truth, then we should do our best to tell the whole of it, to not give the impression that kindness and forgiveness don't coexist with anger and acrimony.

When I had lunch with Freeman, his four words of instruction didn't strike me as particularly wise. Now, I recognize them as the best advice I've ever received. For 22 years at The Times-Picayune—as an intern on the West Bank, a crime and courts reporter in the River Parishes and St. Tammany, as an editorial writer and then a columnist—I've made telling the truth my goal. And telling it with artistry.

This is the last column. NOLA.com and The Times-Picayune have been bought by the owners of The Advocate, and though the new management reached out to me to stay, I decided it was time to move on. I've now lived in New Orleans most of my life. Leaving this place won't be easy. My wife and daughter have shed copious tears at the thought of relocating—even though my new job is in my wife's hometown, and my daughter will get to live near grandparents. New Orleans is our home, and I can't imagine it ever feeling like something other than home.

In December 2017, Vulture.com published an interview with jazz musician Sonny Rollins, who is, as the title of his 1956 album declares, a "Saxophone Colossus." Rollins, who was 87 then, talked about how a diagnosis of pulmonary fibrosis had forced him to put down the horn he'd played so brilliantly for 66 years. Despite having been awarded multiple Grammys, a Guggenheim Fellowship, a Kennedy Center Honor and a National Medal of Arts, Rollins said of his music, "I never got it to where I wanted it to be."

My eyes popped. How could Rollins feel that way?

But then it made sense. If you feel you've reached the top, then there's no need to keep going, no need to try to get better, and Rollins, even at 87 and even with a condition that made it hard to breathe, wanted to be better. "I wanted to be able to play anything that I thought of," he said.

I've worked as a full-time journalist for a third as long as Rollins played sax, and if I am blessed to write as long as he played, I suspect I'll be still trying to get better. In my head—that is, before I write it—every column sounds perfect, but for each one that's been published, I can find something I wish I'd done better.

Though I moved to New Orleans at age 21, it's still accurate to say I grew up here. I'm a better writer because of readers who engaged me, pushed me, even criticized me and blasted my ideas. I'm a better writer because of the people—too numerous to name—who repeatedly encouraged me to tell the truth during those times when I really wanted to play it safe.

That's something Freeman, who died five years after our lunch meeting, forgot to tell me. Telling the truth can be scary.

But not as scary as the thought of not telling it.

JARVIS DEBERRY INTERVIEW

Kalamu ya Salaam: What I'd like to do is talk a bit about two of your decisions: One, to be a writer, which in your case meant starting as a journalist but also doing poetry and creative writing. Two is your decision after Katrina to stay in New Orleans, when at that point you had been part of a team that won a Pulitzer and had offers—and if not strict offers, opportunities in a number of places—and decided to stay here in a situation that arguably was not accommodating at that time period to be a journalist, although there was so much to write about.

Jarvis DeBerry: Correct. I don't know which order I'll take those questions in.

Salaam: I'll give them to you, feed them to you one at a time. I just wanted to let you know that's what I'm going to do. If I remember correctly, you went to Washington University in St. Louis, right?

DeBerry: Yes.

Salaam: You're from Mississippi. What compelled you to go to Washington?

DeBerry: Good question. I had never heard of Washington University before I was in the eleventh grade. I think they still have one of those reputations of just sending out a lot of stuff. If you get a certain score on a standardized test, certain schools have those lists. I was just getting something from them all the time. Every couple of weeks it seems something was coming from Washington University, and just that kind of campaign caused me to at least pay attention to them. I didn't know where I wanted to go to college. I just knew it wasn't going to be in Mississippi. I didn't even apply to anywhere in Mississippi.

Salaam: Did you apply to any schools in Louisiana?

DeBerry: No. I applied to Morehouse in Georgia and Duke in North Carolina. I think I applied to Cornell, Wash-U [Washington University]. I just knew that I wanted to leave the South. A friend and I traveled to Duke for one of those weekends, and it just felt tense. I had never been in a place where just walking onto their campus felt like there was this spirit of antagonism in the air. People just didn't seem comfortable. I remember talking to some of the black students and one black student in particular saying, we don't even like white people, and I'm like, and you came to Duke. Okay. I don't understand that.

Salaam: You understand white kids at Duke; you don't understand the other part.

DeBerry: Yeah. I don't understand how both of those things went together. By contrast, when I went to visit Washington University, it just felt like a welcoming environment. It felt friendly, and maybe the difference was my parents were able to come, and it felt friendly to them. It was within driving distance of home. It would take me about five hours to get to school. I went to college thinking I was going to do something math or science related. In a very ambitious kind of idea, I thought it was going to be something like biomedical engineering or pre-med. I actually enrolled in the engineering program at Wash-U.

I remember the first day of school where the dean was saying how some people are going to find at the end of the year [that] they're not sure if they want to be engineers or not. I remember thinking, I'm not so sure I want to be an engineer right now. That freshman year experience was very instrumental in the rest of my life and in my becoming a writer. There was an English proficiency exam that was required of all engineering students. Basically the whole idea was that you were to take this test, and if you passed it, you didn't have to worry about taking any English composition courses again. I flunked it, and I was so taken aback. They called me in, and they said, we strongly recommend that you take English composition. I was like, what are you talking about? I had never done less than well in any type of English class or writing assignment.

When I met with the dean, I asked, what is the problem? He said, well, your essays lacked paragraph development. I responded, what are you talking about? He shows me this blue book where I had written these essays, and they were all like one-sentence paragraphs. I said, oh I just worked at my hometown newspaper between high school and college. If you know anything about these smaller town newspapers, you'll see the paragraphs are incredibly short.

Salaam: Easier to edit the stories and to fit whatever requirements.

DeBerry: Yeah, so I had gone right out of high school and worked at my hometown newspaper all summer. Went immediately from there to Wash-U, took this English proficiency exam with still this kind of style in my head. They just weren't buying my response that it was a fluke. They dragged me kicking and screaming into English composition, and I get there and I was like, you know what? This is really what I like doing. All the talk I had made of engineering or science or pre-med, I was always constantly going back to the idea that I would write on the side, or after I do engineering, then I'm going to write.

Salaam: You were choosing a "good Negro" route.

DeBerry: I was. I remember having the conversation with my uncle. My uncle has three degrees, all in political science from Brandeis, and he was like, is this really what you want to do? Engineering is lucrative. I just remember saying, I really want to feel like once I graduate from college that I'm smarter. My definition of smarter was somebody who knew more about the world than when they went in. I could tell that engineering was making me more and more and more narrow. The engineering students didn't talk about anything else except calculus and physics; that's what they had to focus on. I didn't want to leave college and not know what was going on around me.

So I changed my major to English, and really, truth be told, the only jobs I've ever had have been in newspapers.

I worked on my hometown newspaper right out of high school. And a couple of summer breaks. Then during my last semester at Wash-U, I had an internship at the Post-Dispatch. It was essentially an entertainment writing position. Their weekend section was called "Get Out." I wrote for them as an intern.

After graduating from Wash-U, I came to New Orleans. I only applied to The Times-Picayune because this girl I was in love with was going to Dillard, and I said, hey, I've never heard of the Picayune, but here's an internship, so I applied for it. That's what brought me here.

Salaam: I'll tell you my story about writing for publication. At The Black Collegian I did all kinds of things, but one of the things was writing our entertainment section or the reviews or what have you. I got a chance to write record reviews. I was interested in music. The problem was the record reviews were one of the last things that were put into the magazine.

DeBerry: You had to fit them into whatever little space was left over?

Salaam: In this particular case, we had I'd say about three inches of space, and the article I'd written was about four and a half inches. The publisher picked up the copy and a pair of scissors, and he said, if you can make it fit, do it.

DeBerry: Yeah. It teaches you to be a different kind of writer. I remember a couple of music reviews I wrote for the Post-Dispatch. I thought they would give me a word count, but they gave me a character count. "You have a thousand characters." I was like, a thousand characters. Oh wow. How am I supposed to... But that's what you've got to do. One of the things I think that working for those publications does is teach you how to say as much as you can in a limited amount of space, which is not always true for other jobs.

Salaam: Also, how to write in such a way that the whole piece hangs together, but at the same time it could easily be edited, and parts of it could be taken out. And you still wouldn't lose the essence.

DeBerry: Correct. Correct.

Salaam: I think I remember you arriving at the Times, but I didn't know the backstory, how you got there. My next question has to do with the specifics. In one story in our workshop, you wrote about a shooting and about covering yourself by squatting down next to a car.

DeBerry: "Engine Blocks and Tire Axles."

Salaam: Yeah, that piece. Because that is not what somebody thinks when one reads in the paper about a shooting.

DeBerry: Yeah.

Salaam: But that was one of the first things you were taught to do when you were covering a shooting.

DeBerry: If there was one story that describes my journalism career in a nutshell, it would be that one. Before

I left St. Louis I requested a meeting with Greg Freeman, who was a columnist with the Post-Dispatch. I
told him that I was nervous. I was going to New Orleans. I was going to be an intern, and it probably meant
I was going to be writing on the crime desk, and I was
going to be writing a lot of crime stories, and I was
concerned about writing stories that would make black
people look bad. What should I do? Greg chuckled and
he said, you tell the truth. I just sat there and said, huh.

The "Engine Blocks and Tire Axles" story is about me
sensing that I'm in physical danger and sensing that the
cops can shoot me accidentally, or the person they're
looking for can fire a bullet that comes my way. But it's
also about what we tell and don't tell in crime stories.
Do you want to know that one black man shot another
black man, or do you want to know that their mothers
hugged each other afterwards? Do you want to know
about this conversation that the women who raised
these young men had? Do you want to know about the
young girl on roller skates rolling past this scene as if
it's completely routine and not even worthy of her attention? Do you want to know all of that?

I don't know if readers have ever been given an opportunity to decide whether or not they would appreciate knowing that.

Salaam: Or to be taught that if you're on the scene of a
shooting, you should hide behind the engine block or
the tire axle because a door or a window doesn't stop
a bullet.

DeBerry: Don't crouch behind the door. I don't think
that the average reader appreciates enough the scenes

that journalists find themselves in. There are all sorts of assumptions made about what a life of ease we must have. But journalists are often in some dicey situations, not just the crime stories but even reporting for Katrina. It's ironic that during Katrina we would tell people to get out even as we were staying behind to report on what was happening. I mean, somebody has to tell those stories, and somebody has to be there.

Salaam: Was there ever a point post-Katrina when you were saying to yourself, I don't know. I don't see how this city is ever going to get back together?

DeBerry: Sometimes, I still feel that, truth be told. New Orleans, for a while there, was so broken and so dark and so desolate and so dysfunctional, more dysfunctional than usual. I really wondered about it all. But at the same time I felt oddly defensive of this city. When you asked me why I remained here, I think that's the primary reason, that for whatever reason being a New Orleanian had become part of my identity.

It's something that I embrace as part of who I am. That didn't happen easily. I felt disconnected from the city for at least the first couple of years I was here. I think NOMMO [a writing workshop for black writers that ran from 1995-2005] was a really big part of me feeling like I had finally established a community in New Orleans. I was just having a conversation with someone last week. He's from Lafayette, white guy from Lafayette. He was talking about how he still hangs out with all the friends he made in first grade. They have now mostly moved to New Orleans, and they all hang out. He knows another group of people in New

Orleans who all grew up in Mobile, and that's like their entire circle. People in New Orleans, it seems, have these friendships that started in first grade. They don't ever change. They go to the same school, same churches, same et cetera.

New Orleans initially felt like a place that would never let me in and felt like a place that could not be easily accessed as an outsider. My participation in NOMMO and also joining Christian Unity Baptist Church were both the primary events that gave me a sense of community because without those two, I probably would never have really formed an attachment to the city. But both of those were communities that actually made me feel welcomed and at home. By the time Katrina came, it felt like, well, this is a place worth defending.

The first column I wrote after Katrina, I mentioned a night when we were at NOMMO, and there was a second line that was going down, and you went out to see who it was for. It was a homeless man that they had found behind one of the funeral homes. It must have been Charbonnet Funeral Home.

I just remember that workshop night, and I remember the thought of a community holding a parade for a homeless man. That so fascinated me, like this is a place where this man would not be overlooked, forgotten, stepped over, ignored like in so many other places. In this city, people say, no, this brother needs to be sent off, and we need to show that he was a part of us even if he was homeless. I mentioned this in the very first column after Katrina in an attempt to explain why people were grieving the loss of their city the way that they were and why people had the audacity to defend this

place. I think we have this image of the American city
as being kind of cold and hostile.

Salaam: The city on the hill.

DeBerry: There are no neighbors, nobody looks out for
one another. There's this coldness and brusqueness and
"every man for himself" kind of attitude. I think people
needed to know that New Orleans was different in that
regard. I worry a lot now about the rapid changes that
we can see in the city. Kelly [Jarvis' wife] and I moved
into our house. We're near Claiborne and Calhoun.

When we moved in, there was this old grandmother
who lived right next to us, and she had two or three
children and, I don't know exactly how many, maybe
four or five grandchildren. Both sides of a double, the
same family, in and out all the time. Sometimes noisy,
but okay, whatever. Then she died, and I don't know if
they just decided to all sell or what the decision was,
but the house got put on the market. A kind of mid-
dle-aged white guy bought it. Right across the street
there were two empty lots. Now there are two doubles
with mostly Tulane med students. In the space of seven
years, six years, the whole character of the neighborhood flipped, just like that. Just with the disappearance
of this one multi-generational black family. I just see
that happening all across the city.

Salaam: Well, it's becoming a typical big city.

DeBerry: Yeah, and so heaven forbid a hurricane hits
15, 20 years from now. I don't know that a columnist
could write the same column about a parade for a

homeless man or those kinds of very neighborly stories that I could write in the beginning of the 21st century.

Salaam: What were your models as a writer? Have you read any kinds of stories you wanted to tell that somebody had written? It could have been about horses, it could have been about apple orchards. But it was the way they wrote it that got to you. Or it could be a mechanic working on cars.

DeBerry: Yeah. I figured you were going to ask me a question like that, so I should have a better answer than I do. Let me start with my grandmother, who wasn't a writer but I think is largely responsible for that branch of my family loving words and loving the sound of words. This is my maternal grandmother. As I put it in a poem, she kept a first aid kit of poetry in her head. She had all these poems memorized. She could remember lines of plays and recitations that she had had to make when she was a girl, like 10 or 12. That kind of love of language, I think, started there. I'm trying to think, who are the newspaper people that I really liked?

When I got here I started reading Leonard Pitts, who works out of Miami. I said, wow, I really like this guy. He writes in a way that I really, really wanted to write, a way that was engaging and welcoming and that seemed open to conversation.

At one point I really admired James Gill [a longtime New Orleans newspaper columnist]. I still have an appreciation for him, but I've just come to the realization that, number one, I can't be him, and number two, that there are things that he does that I shouldn't really aspire to. What I mean by that is that I have felt at times that he can write with absolutely no accountability. He doesn't have to go to church on a Sunday morning after he's written a column and face people who might be disappointed in a position that he has taken. It seems as if he can write with this "people be damned" kind of attitude. I realize that I don't really want that anymore. As much as I crave an independence and a voice and the space to write what I want and think and feel and believe, at the same time I want there to be some people who can say, hey, Jarvis, I don't know about that, or did you consider this?

Salaam: Or ask you why'd you write about him?

DeBerry: Yeah, yeah. You know, at a certain point I felt envious that I couldn't write with this kind of complete and utter freedom. But I've come to appreciate that there are people who are—I don't want to say counting on me, that makes it a little too significant—but there are people who see me doing work for them or see me as important to them. The elderly black ladies that I see in the grocery store who are like, baby, you just keep doing what you doing. I can't disappoint them. I can't write things that would hurt them. There may be things that I write that they disagree with, but I don't want to ever become the writer where I am oblivious to their existence.

Salaam: Callous about their attitude.

DeBerry: Yeah, yeah. When I have talked to young students about opinion writing, my primary assignment has been for them to bring me a column that they think is well written but that they disagree with. I'm trying to have them uncouple this idea that a good column has the position that I agree with, right? Towards that end I would often bring Charles Krauthammer, who just died earlier this year. I don't know that there is any column of his that I ever agreed with on the opinions that were being expressed. But I was often in awe of just how...

Salaam: How he put it together.

DeBerry: ...as beautifully punctilious as you can be. He could present his argument in a way that I thought was very technically sound and proficient and beautiful. Again, I would say I don't agree with it, but damn, that was a good column. You know? I try to pick up things from just about everybody. I've tried to increasingly bring all parts of me to the column, including some humor, including some rage. Trying to be as best as I can, a complete kind of writer. It's still something that I'm learning to do. It's still a learning process.

Other Titles from Runagate Press
An Imprint of University of New Orleans Press

Louisiana Midrash
Marian D. Moore (2019)

New Orleans Griot: The Tom Dent Reader
Tom Dent, Author and Kalamu ya Salaam, Editor (2018)

Be About Beauty
Kalamu ya Salaam (2018)

Previously Published from Runagate Press

Spherical Woman
Kysha Brown Robinson (2009)

From a Bend in the River: 100 New Orleans Poets
Kalamu ya Salaam, Editor (1998)

Fertile Ground: Memories & Visions
Kalamu ya Salaam and Kysha N. Brown, Editors (1996)

Upon the Shoulders of Elephants We Reach the Sky:
A Parents Farewell to a Collegian
Mtumishi St. Julien (1995)

Published by Black Words Press (now Black Academy
Press) in Association with Runagate Press

360° A Revolution of Black Poets
Kalamu ya Salaam, Editor, with Kwame Alexander (1998)